SEE & EXPLORE
LIBRARY

THE
EARTH
and HOW IT WORKS

Written by
Steve Parker

Illustrated by
Giuliano Fornari
Luciano Corbella

DORLING KINDERSLEY, INC.
LONDON · NEW YORK · STUTTGART

DK

A DORLING KINDERSLEY BOOK

Editor Susan Berry

Art Editor Steven Wooster

Series Art Editor Roger Priddy

Series Editor Angela Wilkes

Managing Editor Vicky Davenport

Editorial Consultant Sue Rigby

Revised American Edition, 1993
10 9 8 7 6 5 4 3 2 1

Published in the United States by
Dorling Kindersley, Inc., 232 Madison Avenue
New York, New York 10016

Copyright © 1989
Dorling Kindersley Limited, London

ISBN 1-56458-235-3

Library of Congress Catalog Card
Number 92-54317

Phototypeset by SX Composing Ltd, Rayleigh, England
Reproduced in Singapore by Colourscan
Printed in Spain by Artes Graficas, Toledo S.A.
D.L.TO:1783–1992

CONTENTS

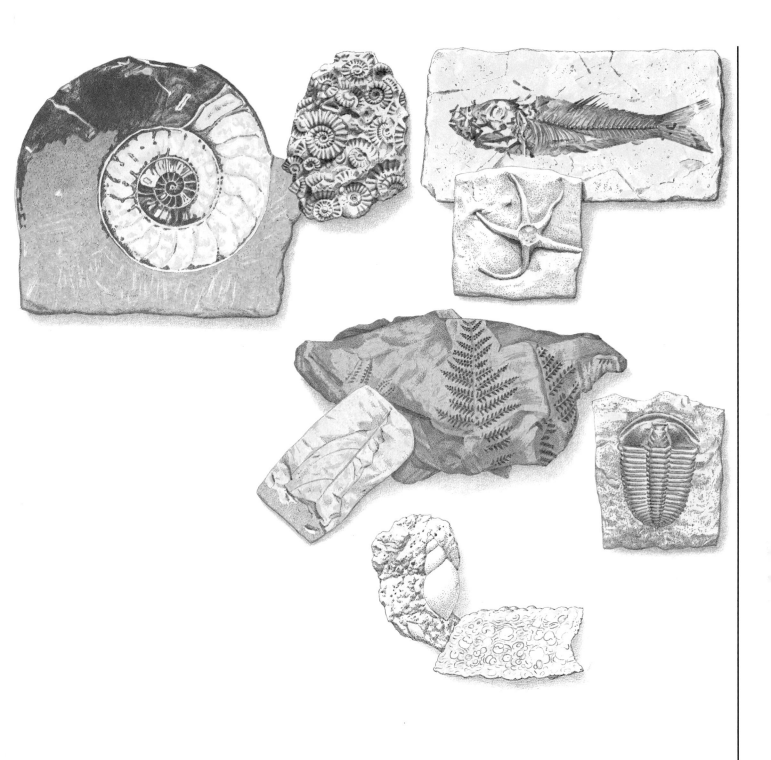

THE EARTH'S AMAZING LANDSCAPE

What is big and spectacular? A movie on the "big screen," perhaps? A rock concert with laser lighting at a stadium for 50,000 people? None of these artificial spectacles bears any comparison with the natural wonders of our planet, the Earth. The problem is that the Earth is so big, and its scenery so vast, that we have trouble picturing it. The facts about the Earth are just as hard to take in. The Earth is about 7,600 miles (12,700 km) in diameter: an excavator digging a hole at one yard per minute would take 24 years to reach the other side. The equator, around the middle of the Earth, is about 25,000 miles (40,000 km); traveling at 65 miles (110 km) an hour, it would take about 16 days to drive around the Earth. The Earth's weight is almost 6,000 million, million, million tons. And its age, 4.6 billion years, almost defies imagination. If the Earth had formed one year ago, all of recorded human history would be packed into the last minute.

Earth spectacular
These are just a few of the world's natural spectacles – most of them have been around for millions of years. But even a million years is a short time in the history of the Earth – equivalent to only two hours in one year. Nothing, not even a giant rock, lasts forever.

Sacred rock
The Earth's largest single rock is Uluru (also known as Ayers Rock) in Australia. Made of reddish stone, it measures 3.6 miles (6 km) long by 1.2 miles (2 km) wide, and is 383 miles (348 m) high. It is a place sacred to the Aboriginals.

Chimney Rock
The 330-foot-high (100 m) Chimney Rock, on the plains of Nebraska, is visible 30 miles (50 km) away. The surrounding rock was worn down by rushing water over the past 2 million years.

Frozen waterfalls
At Hamman-Meskoutine, Algeria, 10 hot-water springs bubble up, carrying many dissolved minerals. Over many centuries, they have built a "frozen waterfall."

The Matterhorn
First climbed in 1865, Europe's Matterhorn 14,777 feet (4,478 m high) is one of the most famous mountains on Earth. Its sides have been gouged and shaped by glaciers for over 2 million years.

Guilin Karst
In Guilin, south China, there is a huge area of high, humpbacked limestone hills, 330 feet (100 m) or more tall, separated by deep ravines.

Mount Fuji
A volcano 12,461 feet (3,776 m) high, Mount Fuji lies about 60 miles (100 km) southwest of Tokyo, Japan. It has a crater 2,310 feet (700 m) across at the summit, and a base 24 miles (40 km) wide.

Devil's Tower
In Wyoming, Devil's Tower looms 875 feet (265 m) above its surroundings. It is a stump of hard rock pushed up 50 million years ago.

Waterless waves
Long ridges of red sand, piled by the wind, look like giant waves in a waterless sea. This is the Arunta (Simpson) Desert in Australia. Some ridges are 100 feet (30 m) high.

Urgup Cones
The Urgup Cones are a strange collection of small hills, some 330 feet (100 m) high, in southeast Turkey. Caps of hard volcanic rock top some of the cones.

Las Marismas
"The Marshes" mark the mouth of the Guadalquivir River in southwest Spain. Coastal water currents have partly blocked the estuary to create a vast wetland of marshes, channels, and islands.

Our changing Earth
Some mountain ranges and parts of the seabed do not alter for millions of years. Yet whole areas of the Earth change in days, or less. In a few hours, two-thirds of the island of Krakatoa was blown to pieces in the biggest volcanic explosion in modern times. Shown here are a few glimpses of the immense power of nature.

Exploding island
In 1883, Krakatoa, an island between Sumatra and Java, erupted in a series of colossal volcanic explosions. The noise was heard 2,400 miles (4,000 km) away and tsunamis (seismic sea waves) 116 feet (35 m) high killed 36,000 people. Krakatoa's volcano has since regrown.

Sheer ice
Icebergs the size of countries crack away from glaciers around the poles (see pages 46-47). One measured 200 miles (335 km) long and 60 miles (100 km) wide – bigger than Belgium.

Lowest spot on Earth
The lowest land on our planet is the shores of the Dead Sea, 1,320 feet (400 m) below sea level. The bed of the lake is the same distance again downward. The salts in the water are about seven times more concentrated than in ordinary seawater.

6

All over in a flash
Around the Earth, lightning leaps from thunderclouds to the ground and back again about 100 times each second. A powerful bolt of lightning may be 3.6 miles (6 km) long, containing enough electrical energy to supply a large town for more than a year.

Building with stone
In the shallow tropical seas of the world, tiny coral animals are busy building huge rocky reefs of limestone (pages 50-51). The Great Barrier Reef, on Australia's northeast coast, is 1,200 miles (2,000 km) long and covers an area the size of Great Britain.

Sculpted by the sea
Each year, the waves of the English Channel cut away the cliffs in northern France. In living memory, the pattern of headlands, overhangs, archways, and needles has changed several times as a result. (pages 48-49).

THE EARTH IN SPACE

The Universe is made up of millions and millions of galaxies, each one flying through space at incredible speed away from all the others. A galaxy is made up of millions of stars, from relatively small ones – "white dwarfs" – to the immense "supergiants." We know that in one particular galaxy there is an average-sized star, which has nine small planets going around and around it. On the third planet outward from this star, there are many different forms of life. One of them is reading these words. It is you. You are on planet Earth, orbiting the star we call the Sun, in an enormous galaxy named the Milky Way, which itself is almost lost in a Universe so vast we do not know what its limits are.

The Sun and the nine planets orbiting it are called the Solar System. The planets are very different from each other, and it is doubtful that any one of them, except Earth, has life on it. But the chances are that, with so many millions of other stars, there may well be planets that resemble Earth in other galaxies – some perhaps with life, like ours.

How the Solar System began

Hundreds of years ago, people did not know that the Earth was shaped like a ball. They assumed that it was flat, and that the stars circled overhead. They thought that at the edges of the Earth, the seas poured into darkness, where monsters lurked. But in 1543, a Polish astronomer, Nicolaus Copernicus, had the idea that the Earth went around the Sun, and modern astronomy was born. One explanation of how the Solar System began is that a passing star pulled a huge stream or "tide" of matter from the Sun, and that this gradually united to form the planets. A more likely theory is that the Solar System formed from a vast cloud of gas and dust pulled together by the force of gravity (see page 12).

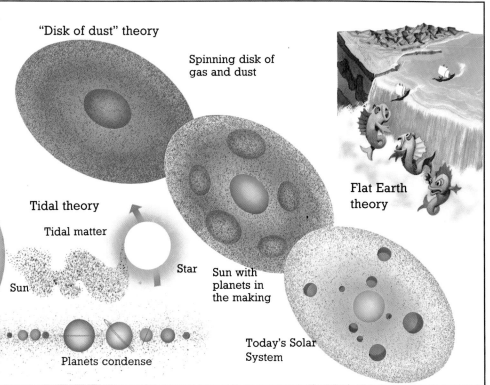

"Disk of dust" theory

Spinning disk of gas and dust

Tidal theory

Tidal matter

Sun

Star

Sun with planets in the making

Planets condense

Today's Solar System

Flat Earth theory

Journey from the Sun
Modern telescopes allow scientists to take clear, close-up photographs of the planets nearest to us. They record X rays and radio and other waves as well as light waves. Spacecraft have landed on the two planets closest to Earth – Mars and Venus – and taken photographs and samples. Other deep-space probes have flown past the seven inner planets with cameras clicking, so we now know much more about our neighbors in the Solar System.

Solar flare, thousands of miles long

Sun

The Sun
The Sun is a burning ball of gases, mainly hydrogen plus a little helium. It is 865,000 miles (1,392,000 km) across – more than a hundred times the diameter of the Earth. The surface temperature is around 10,800°F (6,000°C) – hot enough to burn us even though it's millions of miles away.

Mercury
This innermost and hottest planet in the system is 3,031 miles (4,878 km) across. Only 36 million miles (58 million km) from the Sun, its surface temperatures reach 650°F (340°C). It takes 88 Earth days to go around the Sun.

Mercury

Asteroids

Which planet is biggest?
The planets here
are shown with
their relative
sizes.

Jupiter

Neptune

Saturn

Uranus

Earth

Venus

Pluto

Mercury

Mars

Venus
At 7,520 miles (12,100 km)
across, Venus is much the
same size as Earth. It takes
225 Earth days to orbit the
Sun at a distance of 67
million miles (108 million
km). The surface of Venus
is shrouded in clouds of
carbon dioxide gas.

Asteroids
In the great gap between
Mars and Jupiter are
swarms of tiny planets
called *asteroids*. Scientists
think they may be pieces
of a broken planet, or
(more likely) that they
were formed with the Solar
System and never became
planet size.

Earth
The third planet from the
Sun, 93 million miles (150
million km) away from it,
Earth is 7,926 miles (12,756
km) across. It takes 365
days for the Earth to orbit
the Sun. It is the only
planet with water, and its
surface gases are mainly
nitrogen and the oxygen
that is vital for life. Surface
temperatures vary from
-127°F (-89°C) to more than
136°F (58°C), but the
average is a comfortable
68°F (20°C).

Earth

Venus

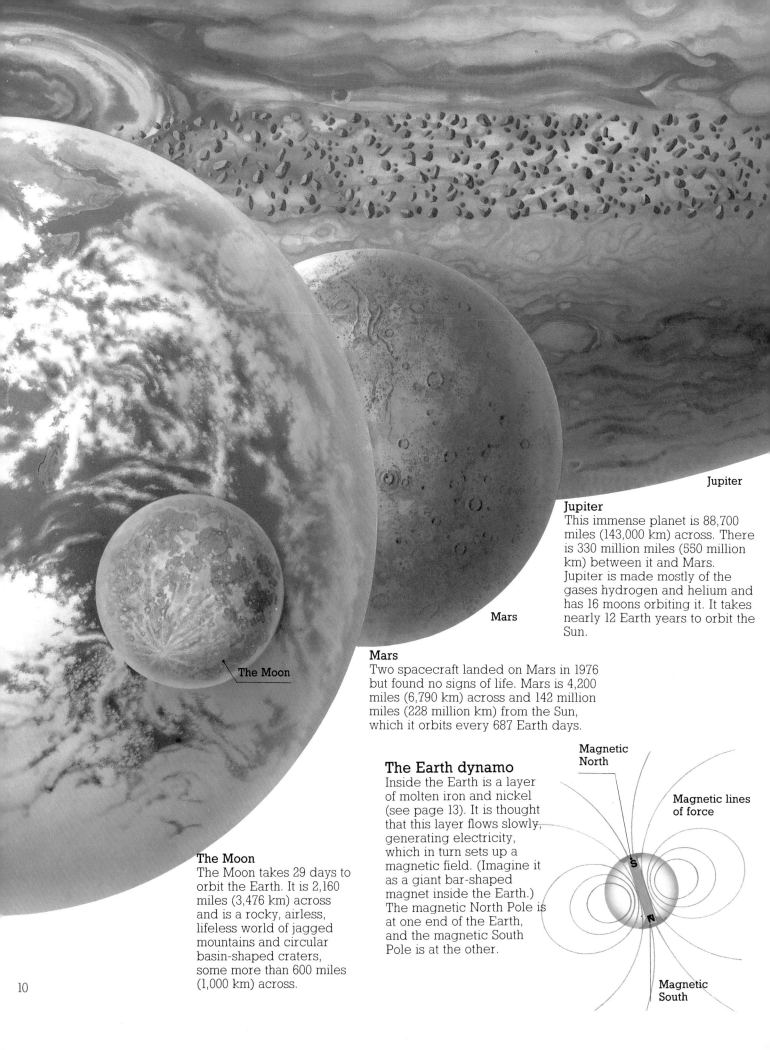

Jupiter
This immense planet is 88,700 miles (143,000 km) across. There is 330 million miles (550 million km) between it and Mars. Jupiter is made mostly of the gases hydrogen and helium and has 16 moons orbiting it. It takes nearly 12 Earth years to orbit the Sun.

Jupiter

Mars

Mars
Two spacecraft landed on Mars in 1976 but found no signs of life. Mars is 4,200 miles (6,790 km) across and 142 million miles (228 million km) from the Sun, which it orbits every 687 Earth days.

The Moon

The Moon
The Moon takes 29 days to orbit the Earth. It is 2,160 miles (3,476 km) across and is a rocky, airless, lifeless world of jagged mountains and circular basin-shaped craters, some more than 600 miles (1,000 km) across.

The Earth dynamo
Inside the Earth is a layer of molten iron and nickel (see page 13). It is thought that this layer flows slowly, generating electricity, which in turn sets up a magnetic field. (Imagine it as a giant bar-shaped magnet inside the Earth.) The magnetic North Pole is at one end of the Earth, and the magnetic South Pole is at the other.

Magnetic North

Magnetic lines of force

Magnetic South

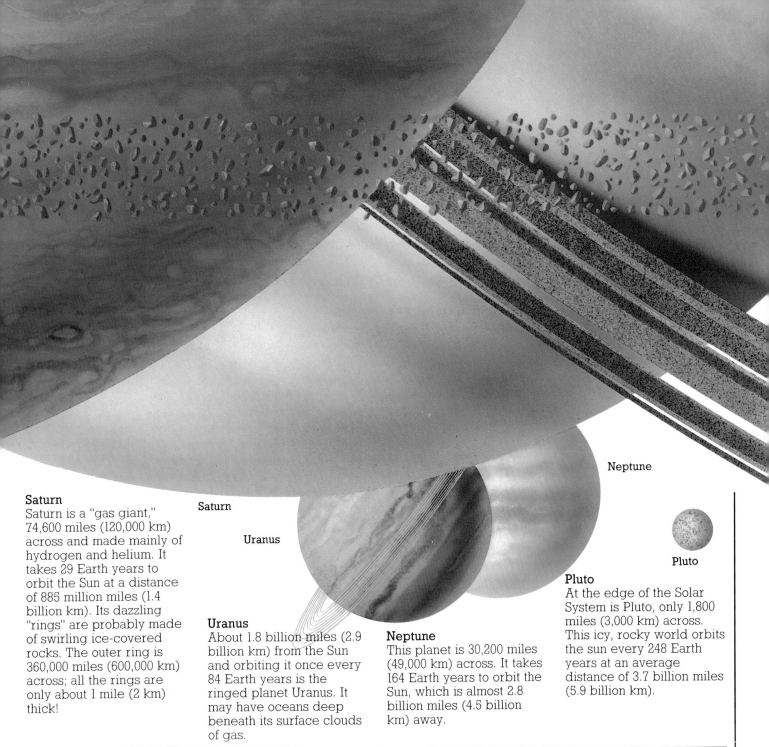

Saturn
Saturn is a "gas giant," 74,600 miles (120,000 km) across and made mainly of hydrogen and helium. It takes 29 Earth years to orbit the Sun at a distance of 885 million miles (1.4 billion km). Its dazzling "rings" are probably made of swirling ice-covered rocks. The outer ring is 360,000 miles (600,000 km) across; all the rings are only about 1 mile (2 km) thick!

Saturn

Uranus

Uranus
About 1.8 billion miles (2.9 billion km) from the Sun and orbiting it once every 84 Earth years is the ringed planet Uranus. It may have oceans deep beneath its surface clouds of gas.

Neptune
This planet is 30,200 miles (49,000 km) across. It takes 164 Earth years to orbit the Sun, which is almost 2.8 billion miles (4.5 billion km) away.

Neptune

Pluto

Pluto
At the edge of the Solar System is Pluto, only 1,800 miles (3,000 km) across. This icy, rocky world orbits the sun every 248 Earth years at an average distance of 3.7 billion miles (5.9 billion km).

Days and seasons
The Earth spins like a top, making one revolution every 24 hours to give us night and day (right). It also goes around the Sun once each year. But the Earth is also tilted by 23.5 degrees. This tilt gives us the seasons, because for six months of the year the upper (northern) part of the Earth leans toward the Sun, and so these months are warmer. Then the lower (southern) part leans toward the Sun, making it warmer there.

Earth

Night

Day

Sun

Moon

Spinning of Earth causes day and night

Earth's orbit around Sun

11

DOWN INTO THE CENTER OF THE EARTH

Telescopes and spaceships have told us much about what is in the skies above our planet. But what is actually under our feet? What is our planet made of? Holes have been drilled far down in the Earth, but even the deepest of these reaches only 8 miles (13 km) below the surface – just about one-thousandth of the way through to the center of the Earth. Fortunately, scientists can make good guesses about what is deep down inside our planet by studying *seismic* waves – the shock waves from earthquakes and underground explosions. Seismic waves travel at certain speeds, and they are bent in specific ways according to the material they are traveling through. Seismic studies indicate that the Earth has four main layers: the crust on the outside, the mantle below

this, then the outer core, and the inner core at the center. Studies of Earth rocks and also Moon rocks, as well as information about other planets, show that the whole Solar System formed at the same time. Our Earth is about 4.6 billion years old.

You may wonder how it is that as the Earth spins around, we do not fly off into space. The answer is the basic laws of physics that say that any object attracts or "pulls on" another object. This force is called *gravity*. Most everyday objects' gravity is too weak to be felt, but the enormous Earth exerts a strong pull of gravity and draws objects toward it, as Sir Isaac Newton realized in the 17th century when an apple fell on his head!

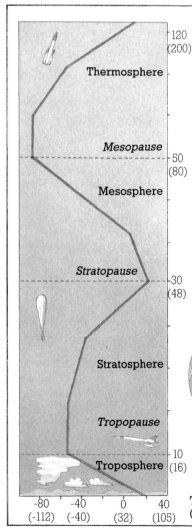

The atmosphere
Around the Earth is the *atmosphere* – the air we breathe - held by the force of gravity. It contains less and less oxygen the higher you go; above 90 miles (150 km) there is none. Climbers of very high mountains need oxygen tanks to breathe comfortably. The atmosphere is divided into four main layers (whose names end with "-sphere"), depending on the air temperature. Airplanes fly and clouds occur in the lowest layer.

Thermosphere

Mesopause

Mesosphere

Stratopause

Stratosphere

Tropopause

Troposphere

120 (200)

50 (80)

30 (48)

10 (16)

Height in miles (kilometers)

-80 (-112) -40 (-40) 0 (32) 40 (105)

Temperature in °Fahrenheit (°Celsius)

The Earth – outside-in
Compared to the whole Earth, the rocks of the crust, which make up our continents and ocean floors, are thinner than the skin on an apple. If the Earth was a model about 83 feet (25 m) across, as shown here, the crust would still be only a few inches thick. And the planet is not a perfect sphere. The diameter at the equator is 26 miles (43 km) greater than it is at the poles.

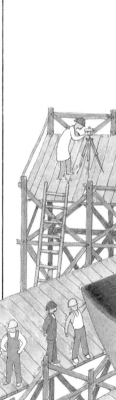

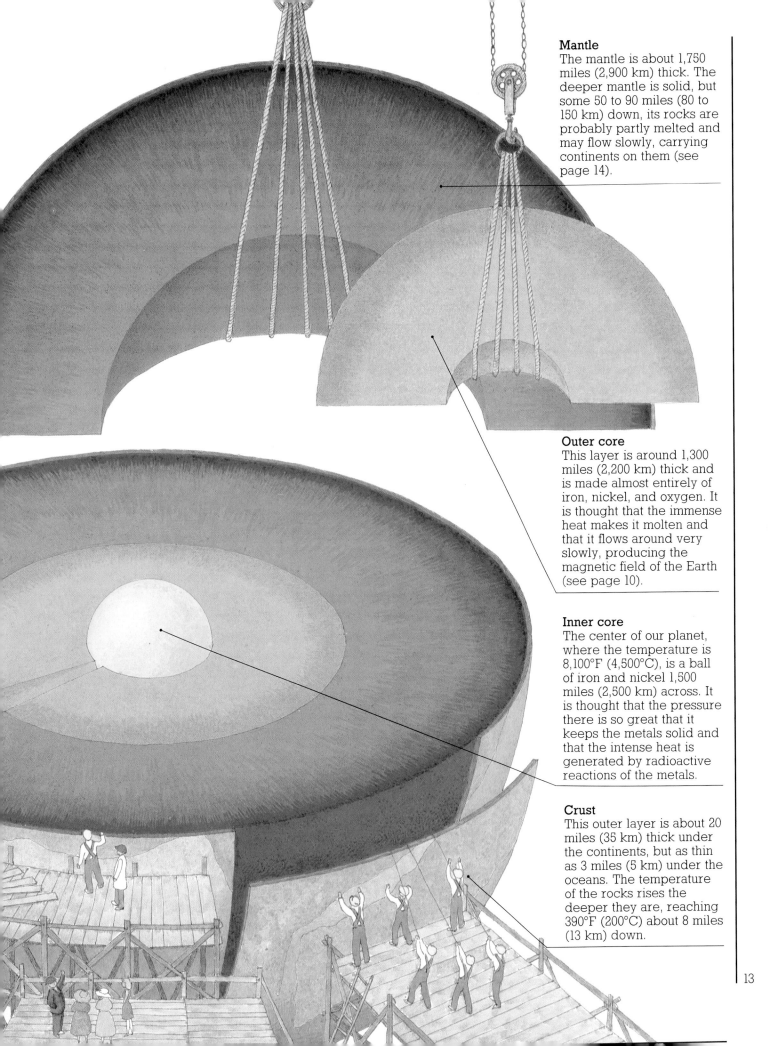

Mantle

The mantle is about 1,750 miles (2,900 km) thick. The deeper mantle is solid, but some 50 to 90 miles (80 to 150 km) down, its rocks are probably partly melted and may flow slowly, carrying continents on them (see page 14).

Outer core

This layer is around 1,300 miles (2,200 km) thick and is made almost entirely of iron, nickel, and oxygen. It is thought that the immense heat makes it molten and that it flows around very slowly, producing the magnetic field of the Earth (see page 10).

Inner core

The center of our planet, where the temperature is 8,100°F (4,500°C), is a ball of iron and nickel 1,500 miles (2,500 km) across. It is thought that the pressure there is so great that it keeps the metals solid and that the intense heat is generated by radioactive reactions of the metals.

Crust

This outer layer is about 20 miles (35 km) thick under the continents, but as thin as 3 miles (5 km) under the oceans. The temperature of the rocks rises the deeper they are, reaching 390°F (200°C) about 8 miles (13 km) down.

THE RESTLESS EARTH

The outside of the Earth is not one continuous piece like the shell of an egg. It is split into seven giant, jagged-edged pieces called *lithospheric plates.* Each plate is curved (rather like a dinner plate) to fit the spherical shape of the Earth. There are also a dozen or so smaller plates – "smaller" meaning that they are only a few thousand miles across.

Each plate is made up of a thin portion of crust and a thicker portion of the outer mantle that lies beneath it (page 13). The seven two-layered plates together form a layer around the Earth called the *lithosphere.* Its average thickness is about 60 miles (100 km). Rocks in the part of the mantle immediately below the lithosphere, called the *asthenosphere,* are at such high temperatures and pressures that they are partly melted. So the lithosphere plates "float" on the asthenosphere. And float they do, because vast forces from within the Earth carry the plates very slowly around the globe in an ever-changing, ball-shaped jigsaw. Over millions of years, the plates bump together, overlap, and slide past each other, in the process making new areas of seabed, building mountains, and causing volcanoes and earthquakes (see pages 20-25).

Wandering continents

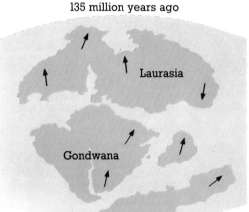

135 million years ago

Laurasia

Gondwana

65 million years ago

North America Europe and Asia

Africa

South America India

Antarctica

About 200 million years ago, there was just one supercontinent on Earth called Pangaea. Slowly, this split into two parts: Laurasia, which drifted north, and Gondwana, which went south. Gradually, each of these split again, until seven great land masses were formed. These *continents* have drifted an inch or so each year, (and still do) to make the familar map of the world we know today (see pages 62-63).

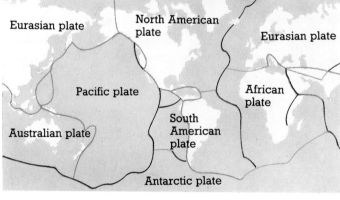

Eurasian plate North American plate Eurasian plate

Pacific plate African plate

Australian plate South American plate

Antarctic plate

——— Plates being made

——— Plates sliding past

——— Plates being destroyed

The making of island mountains
If you could make a slit about 120 miles (200 km) long in the Earth, somewhere near Japan, you might see a scene like the one below. The Pacific plate, moving in from the left, is gradually being forced under the Eurasian plate. The volcanic island chain of Japan marks their meeting. As the edge of the Pacific plate goes under, it forms an oceanic trench 6 miles (10 km) below sea level. Some plates have only oceanic crust (like the Pacific plate); some carry only continental crust (page 18); and some have both types.

Melting in the mantle
As the oceanic part of the plate tilts under the continental plate, it causes earthquakes many miles down. Its rocks melt in the rising temperature of the mantle. This molten *magma* is under incredible pressure and forces its way upward through holes and cracks.

The world today, showing the main lithospheric plates

Pushing up islands
Magma, molten rock from deep in the crust, pours up through cracks to the surface and becomes *lava*, the molten rock coming out of a volcano. Repeated eruptions over millions of years gradually build a line of volcano-topped islands.

Going down
As the thin oceanic part of the Pacific plate moves toward the thicker continental plate, it is forced down into the mantle. This is the *subduction zone*. On the seabed there is a deep trench, thousands of yards below sea level, where the oceanic plate disappears downward.

Under the ocean
The oceanic crust is about 3 to 6 miles (5 to 10 km) thick; in the deepest oceans, it is covered by the same depth again of water. The crust, on its plate, moves sideways about 0.4 to 0.8 inches (1 to 2 cm) each year – fast enough to be measured.

At the edges of plates

Collision course
When two continental regions of plates come together, they are both too thick to be pushed back into the mantle. They collide, crack, fold, and buckle to throw up great mountain ranges like the Himalayas (see page 16).

Growing apart
Where oceanic parts of two plates "meet," they are often pushed apart as magma wells up from the mantle, cools, and solidifies into basalt rocks that add to the edge of the plates. This is happening under the Atlantic Ocean (see page 18).

Sliding past
Another type of plate boundary is where two plates rub and slide sideways past each other. No new rocks are created or destroyed, but there is the occasional land-shattering earthquake (see page 20).

Roots of the mountain
Deep under mountains are vast chambers filled with solidified magma, called *batholiths*. The smallest cover 40 square miles (100 sq km). In time, when the mountains wear down, the batholiths may become exposed.

Crusts on the plates
Each lithospheric plate consists of a rigid piece of crust carried on a rigid piece of the outer mantle. The plates are about 42 to 48 miles (70 to 80 km) thick in oceanic areas, and 60 to 90 miles (100 to 150 km) thick in continental areas.

MOUNTAINS IN THE MAKING

Around the world, mountains are being built as the edges of *lithospheric plates* ram into each other. And around the world, mountains are being worn down by snow, rain, wind, and other natural forces. In general, younger mountain ranges like the Alps tend to have sharp peaks and deep valleys. Many millions of years of erosion round off the peaks, as in the Appalachian mountains in North America.

But plate movements are not the only mountain-builders. Volcanic eruptions (see page 22) also make mountains. The world's tallest peak, Mauna Kea, Hawaii, is 33,670 feet (10,203 m) high, measured from the seabed to the tip. Only 13,877 feet (4,205 m) are above sea level. Other mountains are formed when an outcrop of hard rock is left after surrounding rocks have been worn away.

Young and ragged
The Alps of Europe are only a few million years old and not yet worn and rounded by erosion. The range is 600 miles (1,000 km) long, and the tallest peak is Mont Blanc, 15,863 feet (4,807 m) high.

Dome of stone
About 300 million years ago, a lump of molten rock tried to force its way upward from 10,000 feet (3,000 m) below the surface. The "lump" is known as Stone Mountain, 828 feet (251 m) high, in the state of Georgia.

Rocks on high
These mountains from across the world come in various shapes and sizes, reflecting the different ways in which they formed. The highest point on the Earth's surface is the summit of Mount Everest in the Himalayas, which towers 29,198 feet (8,848 m) above sea level.

Earth's greatest mountains
The Himalayas have been formed in the last 45 million years as India, carried on the Australian lithospheric plate, collided with the Eurasian plate. The world's 20 highest mountains are in this and the adjoining ranges.

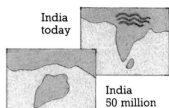

India today

India 50 million years ago

Lichens

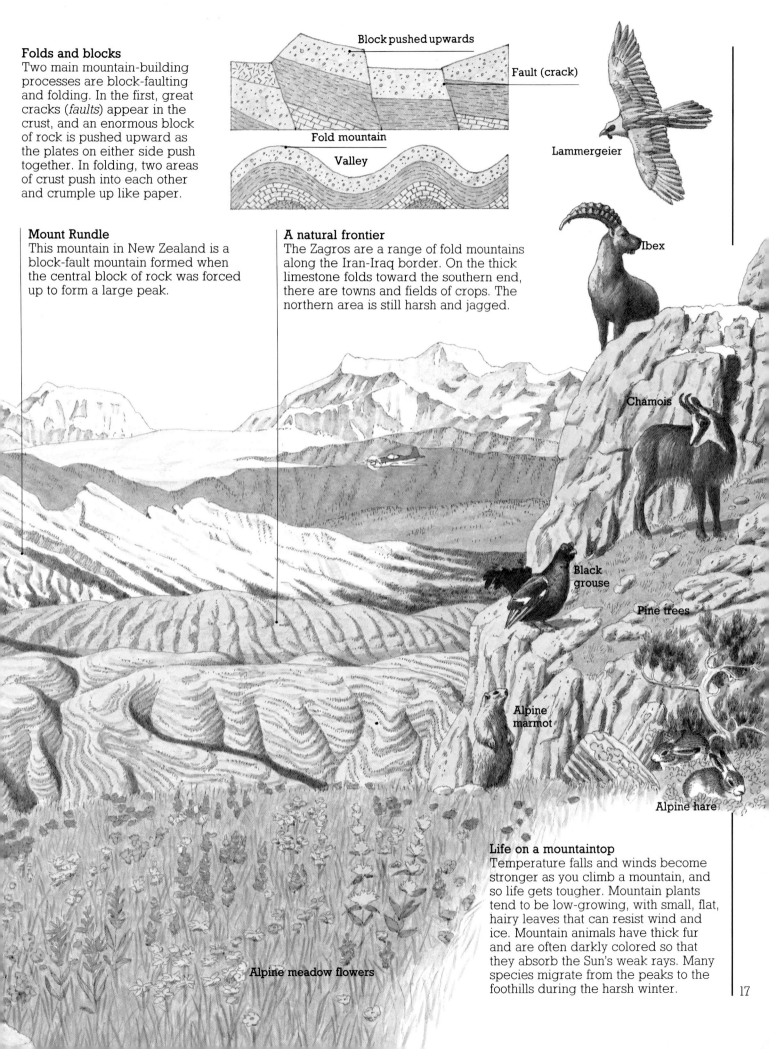

Folds and blocks

Two main mountain-building processes are block-faulting and folding. In the first, great cracks (*faults*) appear in the crust, and an enormous block of rock is pushed upward as the plates on either side push together. In folding, two areas of crust push into each other and crumple up like paper.

Block pushed upwards

Fault (crack)

Fold mountain

Valley

Lammergeier

Ibex

Chamois

Mount Rundle

This mountain in New Zealand is a block-fault mountain formed when the central block of rock was forced up to form a large peak.

A natural frontier

The Zagros are a range of fold mountains along the Iran-Iraq border. On the thick limestone folds toward the southern end, there are towns and fields of crops. The northern area is still harsh and jagged.

Black grouse

Pine trees

Alpine marmot

Alpine hare

Alpine meadow flowers

Life on a mountaintop

Temperature falls and winds become stronger as you climb a mountain, and so life gets tougher. Mountain plants tend to be low-growing, with small, flat, hairy leaves that can resist wind and ice. Mountain animals have thick fur and are often darkly colored so that they absorb the Sun's weak rays. Many species migrate from the peaks to the foothills during the harsh winter.

17

THE OCEAN PROFILE

Oceans cover seven-tenths of our Earth. The largest is the Pacific, with a staggering area of 66 million square miles (165 million sq km) – about one-third of the globe. The ocean's surface may look almost flat, rippled only by waves, but under the water, the ocean floor is a fascinating landscape of flat plains, hills, and jagged mountains. Sometimes tips of mountains rise above the water's surface as islands. There are around 25,000 of them in the Pacific alone.

North America

The Caribbean islands
The 300 islands of Bermuda are the limestone tips of mountains rising from the seabed, 570 miles (950 km) west of North America. The main island, Bermuda, is 14 miles (23 km) long.

Continental crust
The Earth's crust under the land masses – called continental crust – is thicker and has many more different layers than the crust under the Earth's oceans. The oceanic crust was formed more recently than the land – in the last 200 million years.

Like the rest of the Earth, the ocean floor is moving very slowly. An enormous chain of undersea mountains 36,000 miles (60,000 km) long winds through the oceans of the world. Much of it follows the edges of the great lithospheric plates (page 14). It is here that the plates are moving apart in a process called *seafloor spreading*. As they slide apart sideways, molten rock (*magma*) from the mantle rises and cools and solidifes, adding to the edges of the plates. It is a region of volcanoes and earthquakes. The range in the Atlantic (the Mid-Atlantic Ridge) is the greatest of all. Some chains of volcanic islands, such as those in Hawaii, form over "hot spots," or sources of radioactive heat in the mantle, far away from the plate edges. As the plates drift on, the older volcanoes are carried sideways and new ones are created to form a chain of peaks. The oceans were all formed since the breakup of Pangaea. The Atlantic was formed in the last 100 million years.

At the bottom of the sea
The Atlantic Ocean covers one-fifth of the Earth. Under the sea is a central range of mountains with, on either side, higher peaks that break the surface and form islands, such as Bermuda and the Canaries. The deepest part of the Atlantic is the Puerto Rico Trench, near the Caribbean. (The mountains have been drawn taller than they are so that they can be seen more easily.)

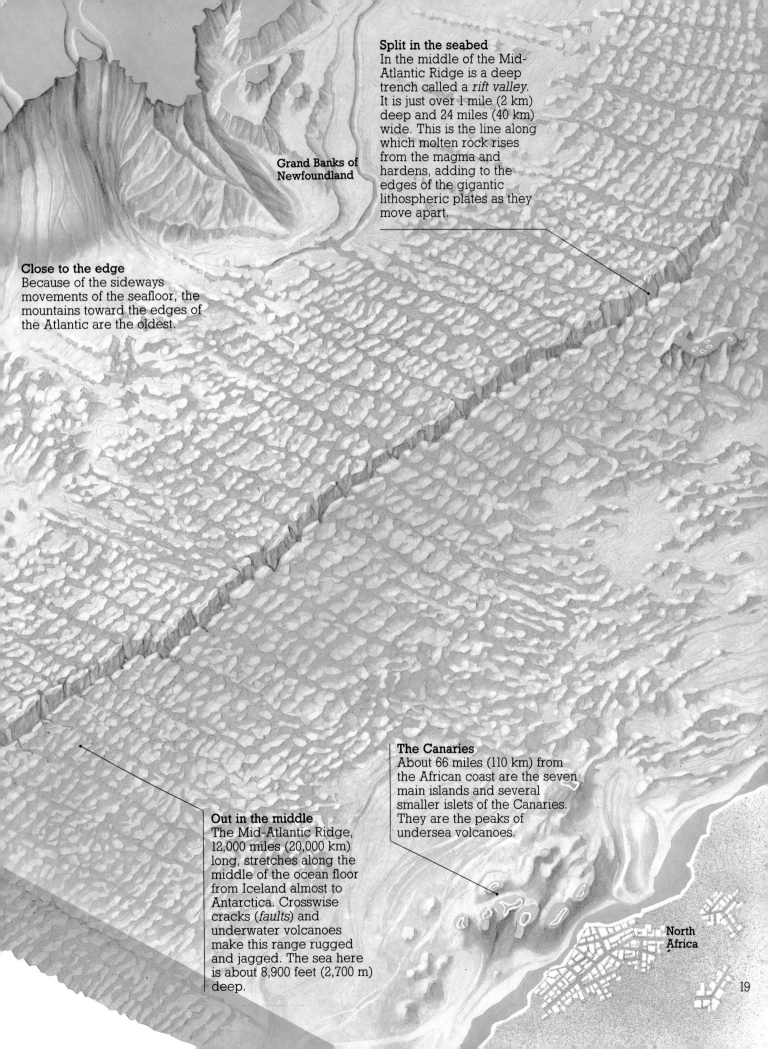

Split in the seabed
In the middle of the Mid-Atlantic Ridge is a deep trench called a *rift valley*. It is just over 1 mile (2 km) deep and 24 miles (40 km) wide. This is the line along which molten rock rises from the magma and hardens, adding to the edges of the gigantic lithospheric plates as they move apart.

Grand Banks of Newfoundland

Close to the edge
Because of the sideways movements of the seafloor, the mountains toward the edges of the Atlantic are the oldest.

The Canaries
About 66 miles (110 km) from the African coast are the seven main islands and several smaller islets of the Canaries. They are the peaks of undersea volcanoes.

Out in the middle
The Mid-Atlantic Ridge, 12,000 miles (20,000 km) long, stretches along the middle of the ocean floor from Iceland almost to Antarctica. Crosswise cracks (*faults*) and underwater volcanoes make this range rugged and jagged. The sea here is about 8,900 feet (2,700 m) deep.

North Africa

19

EARTHQUAKE!

How many earthquakes are there each year around the world? Perhaps 10? Possibly 50? In fact, there may be 100,000 or more, of which about 6,000 are detected by scientific instruments. Of course, most are either too small to do any damage, or they occur in remote areas or under the sea. But about 1,000 cause some sort of damage, and 15 to 20 each year are strong enough to split the ground, topple trees and buildings, and cause great loss of life.

An earthquake is one of the most obvious signs of our restless Earth. Most earthquakes happen at the edges of the giant lithospheric plates (page 14) as these drift across the globe. Where two plates try to move past each other, their jagged edges lock together until, suddenly, the strain is too much. The rocks slip and slide, the ground shakes and cracks, and there may be a deafening roar. Most earthquakes last only seconds or a few minutes. However, their vibrations pass through rocks like ripples from a pebble thrown into a pond. These *seismic waves* travel through and around the Earth, reaching the other side in 20 minutes. Studying them has told us much about what is deep inside our planet (see page 12).

Earthquake damage
In a few places each year, earthquakes devastate buildings and gash open the ground. Holes and cracks several yards wide may open up and swallow cars and buildings. However, these holes are quickly blocked by broken falling rocks, and they are rarely more than a few yards deep.

The wrong side of the street
On the far side of the road, there was hardly a tremble. A firm block of rock lies under here. On the near side, where the slippage and movement occurred, houses and shops were rattled and shaken apart as though made of toy building blocks.

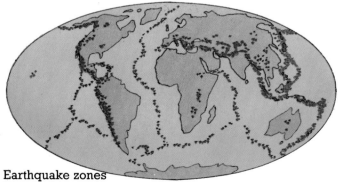

Earthquake zones
The regions where most earthquakes happen closely follow the edges of the Earth's lithospheric plates (page 14). In many earthquakes, the point where most rock movement occurs, the *focus*, is deep below the ground. At the surface, above the focus, the damage is greatest.

The Richter scale
In 1935, the American earthquake expert Charles Richter invented a scale for measuring the strength of the vibrations from an earthquake. A measurement of 4 or more usually causes damage.

Force 1-2
Signs swing, slight trembling

Force 2-3
Liquids spill, definite tremors felt

Living on the fault line
The San Andreas Fault is the place where the Pacific and North American plates slide past each other. The San Francisco earthquake of 1906 was on this fault. Smaller earth movements happen, too; this row of trees has moved sideways from the rest of the orchard.

Force 4
Windows break, walls crack

Force 5
Chimneys topple

Force 6
Ground cracks

Force 7-8
Major damage, railway lines bent

Built to last

People who live in areas where there are frequent earthquakes have learned to take various precautions. For example, some tall buildings are constructed in a pyramid or cone shape. This is a very rigid design, and with its broad base, it is unlikely to topple over in an earthquake.

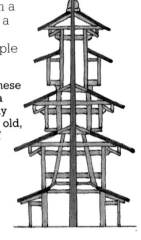

San Francisco's TransAmerica Building has a stable, tapering shape.

The Japanese pagoda, a style many centuries old, has a stiff central column.

An uplifting experience

An earthquake not only shakes the ground, but may also crack and tilt it as one side slips down (*subsides*) and the other pushes up (*uplifts*). A series of such cracks can create a new hillside in a few seconds. After the great Alaskan earthquake of 1964, some parts of the land around Prince William Sound had subsided by 7 yards, while areas of the seabed under the sound rose by more than 8 yards! This earthquake measured 8.3 on the Richter scale.

"Here is an earthquake warning . . ."

Predicting earthquakes is tricky, even with modern *seismometers* that detect the slightest tremors. Here are some earthquake-forecasting devices from ancient times. This Italian seismometer (*below left*), was invented in 1751. During an earthquake, the pendulum grooves the sand in the tray. The Chinese device (*below right*) dates from AD 132. A tremor caused the mouth of one of the dragons to open and a ball to drop out.

Italian seismometer

Chinese dragon device

THE EXPLODING LANDSCAPE

Few sights on our Earth are more awesome than a volcano in action – the earth splits and molten red-hot rocks and ash spew out across the countryside. How does it happen? Deep under the Earth's surface is *magma* – rock at such great temperature that it has melted. In certain parts of the world, the solid rocks of the crust are thin and weak, and the magma presses on the rocks above. Imagine shaking a soda can so the pressure builds up inside. When you pull off the tab, whoosh! A volcano is a bit like that. With colossal force, like that of thousands of tons of TNT, the magma bursts through the weakened rock to the surface. Its explosive exit into the open air is an *eruption*, and it is now called *lava*. Once in the air, it quickly cools and becomes less runny, eventually turning into solid rock of the *igneous* type (see page 26).

In some volcanoes, the lava flows from the opening (*vent*) and gradually hardens, piling layer upon layer. In others, the vent is plugged by hardened lava, and the forces from below build up to many tons per square inch. At last the plug is blown out, and molten rock is hurled high into the air.

When a volcano keeps erupting, we say it is *active*. When it has not erupted for many years, and all seems quiet, it is called *dormant* ("sleeping"). A very old volcano that we are certain will never erupt again is *extinct*.

Mountains made from molten rock
Depending on the minerals it contains, and the temperature and pressure of its formation, lava may be thick and viscous like tar, or thin and runny like engine oil. Often it has gas bubbles in it. The type of lava, the force with which it erupts, and the amount of gas all determine the shape of the volcano. Not all volcanoes are high, cone-shaped mountains. They come in various shapes and sizes. After thousands of years, when volcanoes are worn down, hills often form from the hard rocks that were once in the vent.

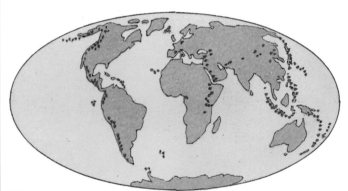

Volcano zones
There are about 500 active volcanoes on land, and many more under the sea (see page 24). They are found mostly along the edges of the Earth's giant lithospheric plates.

Ex-volcano country
Formerly volcanic regions yield strange landscapes. Ship Rock Towers in New Mexico is a "plug" of solidified lava 1,403 feet (425 m) high around the neck of a volcano. Le Puy in France is built on an extinct volcanic cone. Giant's Causeway, on Northern Ireland's coast, is a patchwork of six-sided columns formed when lava cooled.

Le Puy

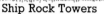

Ship Rock Towers

Spreading sideways
In a *flood basalt* or *shield* volcano, the lava is thin and runny. It wells up gently from a hole or crack and flows outward to form gently sloping hills. In the vast flood basalts of Washington and Oregon, some lavas flowed 90 miles (150 km) from their vents.

Giant's Causeway

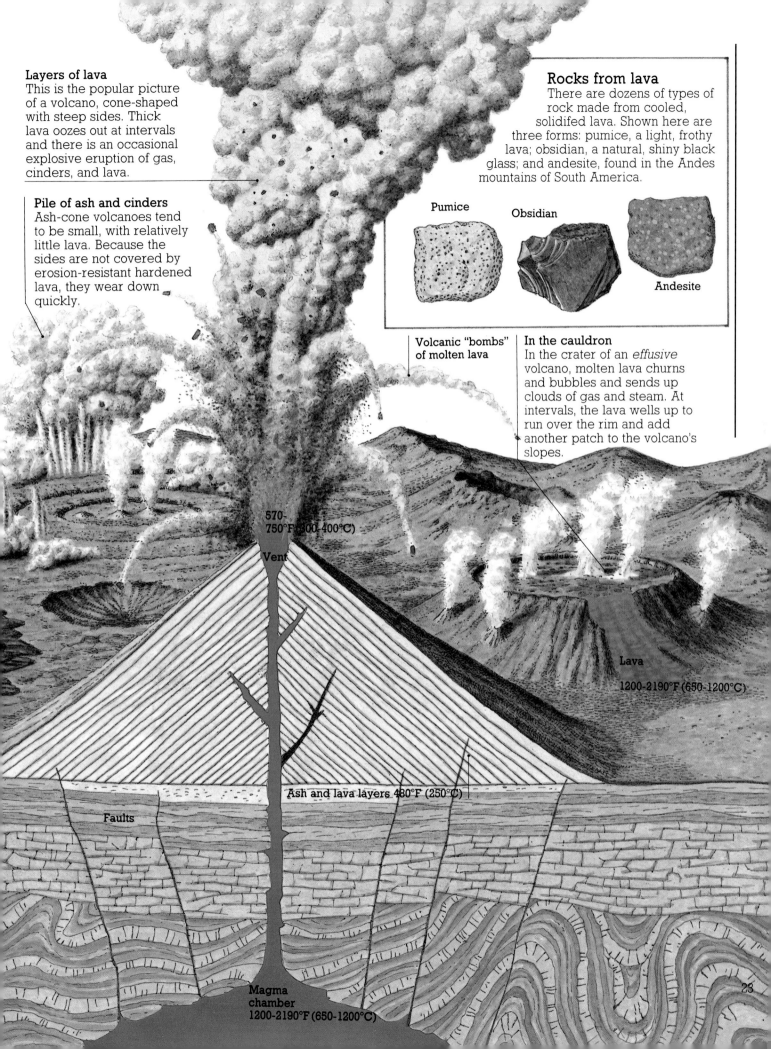

Layers of lava
This is the popular picture of a volcano, cone-shaped with steep sides. Thick lava oozes out at intervals and there is an occasional explosive eruption of gas, cinders, and lava.

Pile of ash and cinders
Ash-cone volcanoes tend to be small, with relatively little lava. Because the sides are not covered by erosion-resistant hardened lava, they wear down quickly.

Rocks from lava
There are dozens of types of rock made from cooled, solidifed lava. Shown here are three forms: pumice, a light, frothy lava; obsidian, a natural, shiny black glass; and andesite, found in the Andes mountains of South America.

Pumice

Obsidian

Andesite

Volcanic "bombs" of molten lava

In the cauldron
In the crater of an *effusive* volcano, molten lava churns and bubbles and sends up clouds of gas and steam. At intervals, the lava wells up to run over the rim and add another patch to the volcano's slopes.

570-750°F (300-400°C)

Vent

Lava
1200-2190°F (650-1200°C)

Ash and lava layers 480°F (250°C)

Faults

Magma chamber
1200-2190°F (650-1200°C)

23

Death of a mountain

Mount St. Helens in Washington lay dormant for 123 years. Then in May 1980, a volcanic eruption blew away one whole side of the mountain, reducing its height by 1,300 feet (400 m).

May 18, 1980

May 19, 1980

The biggest blasts

Volcanic eruptions such as Mount St. Helens and Vesuvius (which destroyed Pompeii in AD 79) are small compared to the gigantic blasts of Tambora and Krakatoa (see page 6).

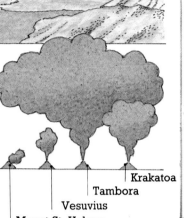

Krakatoa
Tambora
Vesuvius
Mount St. Helens

An island is born

Many islands, such as the Hawaiian group, are the tips of undersea volcanoes (page 18). In 1963, a new volcanic island appeared above the waves 6 miles (10 km) southwest of Iceland. It was christened Surtsey (the name of the Norse fire god). Within one month, scientists went ashore on the steaming lava to study the rocks. After three years, the main activity died down. Surtsey is now about 580 feet (75 m) high; plants and animals thrive there.

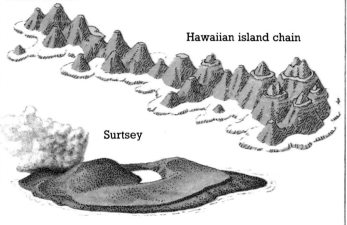

Hawaiian island chain

Surtsey

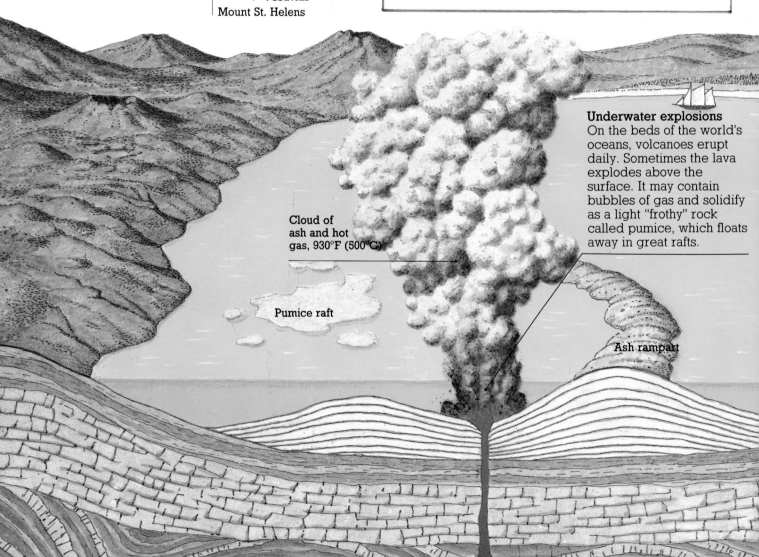

Underwater explosions

On the beds of the world's oceans, volcanoes erupt daily. Sometimes the lava explodes above the surface. It may contain bubbles of gas and solidify as a light "frothy" rock called pumice, which floats away in great rafts.

Cloud of ash and hot gas, 930°F (500°C)

Pumice raft

Ash rampart

1200-2190°F (650-1200°C)

Bubbling mud pots
In New Zealand, Iceland, Japan, and other areas, natural hot-water springs mix with mineral particles and soil to form warm, bubbling mud.

Gushing geysers
In a geyser, water in an underground chamber is heated above its boiling point by molten rock (*magma*) lying close to the Earth's surface. As the pressure builds, the water and steam are finally forced through a hole. They spurt high into the air as a spectacular fountain, releasing the pressurized water and steam. The geyser then dies down, and the process starts again.

Geysers and fumaroles
In Icelandic, geyser means "gusher." And this is exactly what a geyser does, shooting hot water and steam high into the air. The world famous geyser, Old Faithful, in Yellowstone National Park, has been erupting every 30 to 90 minutes for more than a century. Each time, it sends hot water 100 to 165 feet (30-50 m) into the air for up to 5 minutes.

Most geysers are in areas where volcanoes have been active in the past million years or so. The rocks under the surface are still very warm, and they heat rainwater that trickles through to the geyser's subterranean chamber. Most geysers spurt for a few minutes, then lie dormant for a time as the underground water is replenished and heated again. In a fumarole, or "fume hole," hot gases rather than water escape.

In New Zealand, Iceland, Japan, and other places, geysers and hot springs provide a source of energy. In Reykjavík, the capital of Iceland, the central heating for the town is piped from the hot-water geysers.

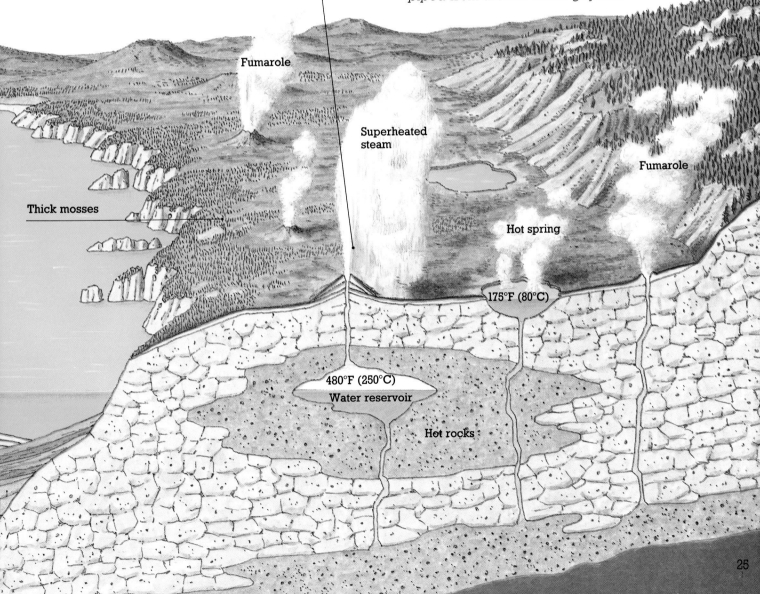

Fumarole

Superheated steam

Thick mosses

Fumarole

Hot spring

175°F (80°C)

480°F (250°C)
Water reservoir

Hot rocks

ROCK OF AGES

Our world is built on layers of rocks that have taken thousands of years to form. If you go down far enough below the Earth's surface, even in the middle of the ocean, you eventually come to rocks – hard substances made from minerals (see below). Their different types and proportions give each rock its particular character – color, texture, hardness, and other features. There are three main types. Igneous ("fiery") rocks were first heated until they melted under the great temperatures and pressures within the Earth, after which they gradually cooled and solidified. Sedimentary rocks were laid down as layers of sand, silt, and mud were squeezed together. Metamorphic ("changed") rocks were formed when temperature, pressure, or chemicals changed the other two types of rock.

Common and colorful rock

You probably think all rocks look the same. They don't. Some are surprisingly colorful, and some contain beautiful minerals (see page 56) that have become very precious. Shown on the right are some of the most common rocks – igneous, metamorphic, and sedimentary – that make up our Earth's crust. Also included are rocks that are especially colorful or useful.

Minerals make up rock

A mineral is a natural, nonliving substance that has a characteristic chemical makeup. Different mixtures of minerals make the various types of rock. Granite, for example, a hard igneous rock, is made of three main minerals. The two most important ones are quartz (crystals of silicon and oxygen) and feldspar (silicon, oxygen, and aluminum). The dark mineral is often mica.

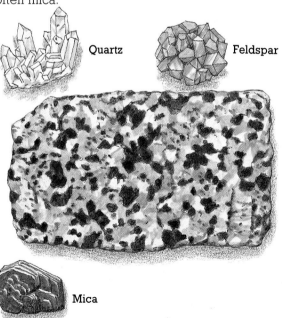

Quartz

Feldspar

Mica

Metamorphic rocks

Slate (*right*)

This dark, heavy rock, like many other metamorphic rocks, splits easily to form thin, flat, strong sheets. Slate is quarried and used for roofs and floors (and old-fashioned chalkboards!).

Hornfels (*left*)

Hard, dense, and often dark green, hornfels is made when certain sedimentary rocks are heated to 930°F (500°C) under great pressure. They melt and then re-solidify into tiny crystals.

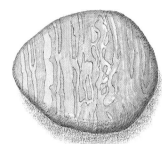

Gneiss (*right*)

A very commonly found rock, gneiss is usually formed in layers of different minerals: feldspar, quartz, garnet, and mica. The proportions of the minerals determine its color.

Mica schist (*left*)

This type of rock may peel into thin sheets, called mica, which is very resistant to electricity and hardly expands when heated. As a result, it is useful for electrical and heat insulation. The glassy surface of mica gives a sparkle to the rock in which it is found.

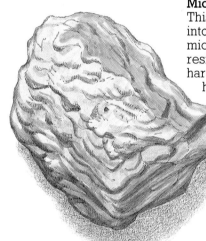

Igneous rocks

Quartz porphyry (*right*)

A porphyry is a rock with large mineral crystals embedded in a mixture of tiny ones. Quartz porphyry also contains quartz crystals (see page 56).

Pegmatite (*left*)

A form of coarsely crystallized granite, it often contains very large crystals of quartz, feldspar, and mica, sometimes yards long. Precious stones such as topaz (see page 57) are sometimes found in it.

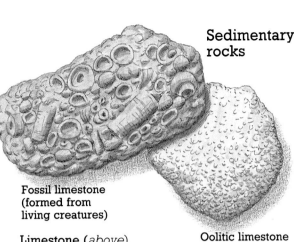

Sedimentary rocks

Fossil limestone (formed from living creatures)

Limestone (*above*)
There are many forms of limestone, but they all contain *calcium carbonate*. Fossil limestone has shells of animals embedded in it.

Oolitic limestone (formed from nonliving material)

Chalk (*above*)
This is a type of soft limestone, made mostly from tiny pieces of microscopic shelled sea plants.

Quartzite sandstone (*above*)
Unlike arkose, quartzite sandstone is made mostly of the mineral quartz, which forms the grains of ordinary beach sand. The grains are .08 to .0025 inches (2mm to 1/16mm) across.

Arkose sandstone (*above*)
Sandstones are made when sand grains settle and are squeezed together and cemented by other mineral crystals. Arkose sandstone has a mixture of quartz and feldspar minerals.

Tufa (*above*)
This soft, bubble-filled rock is made up mainly of calcite (calcium carbonate). It is deposited from water around hot springs. Ancient Romans used tufa for building.

Ironstone (*above*)
An ironstone is a rock that contains iron. It can be used as an *ore*, from which the iron is extracted and used to make metallic iron and steel. Modern industry depends on iron to make steel for machines, vehicles, bridges, buildings . . .

Flint (*left*)
Prehistoric humans chipped sharp-edged flints to make the first tools and sparks for their fires. It is a dark, dense, hard rock that occurs in rounded lumps.

Shale (*above*)
This is an abundant sedimentary rock. Some shales contain remains of animals and plants. The oil we use today comes from shales (see page 54).

The story of a rock
Chalk is a sedimentary rock formed from particles settling on the seabed. Yet today chalk is found far from the sea. Why? About 100 million years ago, shallow seas covered much of today's continents. Chalky sediments settled in them. Gradually, continents drifted apart (see page 14), and the chalk was carried along. Buckling of the land then lifted the chalk to its present positions.

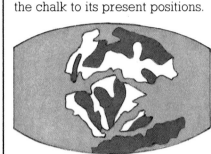

100 million years ago

50 million years ago

Today

THE RECORD IN THE ROCKS

The spectacular steep-sided valley, or gorge, known as the Grand Canyon in northwestern Arizona is one of the natural wonders of the world. Cut into the rocks over thousands of years by the waters of the Colorado River and by winds, it is about 265 miles (440 km) long, and its width varies from about 3.5 to 18 miles (6 to 30 km). In places, it is almost 1 mile (1.5 km) from top to bottom. A 100-mile (170-km) length of the canyon has been made a U.S. National Park. As the river has cut its way downward, it has exposed different layers of rocks that were formerly invisible under the surface. They are mostly sandstones and limestones (see page 27), sedimentary rocks formed when the area was covered by shallow seas millions of years ago. As a result, they contain many fossils of extinct sea creatures (see page 30). Going down the steep trails to the bottom of the gorge is like traveling back in time – the lower you go, the older the rocks.

Canyon of many colors
The layers of rocks in the Grand Canyon are of many colors – the different minerals they contain, like iron and copper, are not removed by weathering. There is little rain here, and the Colorado River is fed by rain falling far east in the Rocky Mountains. The only plants are scrubby thornbushes and a few juniper trees.

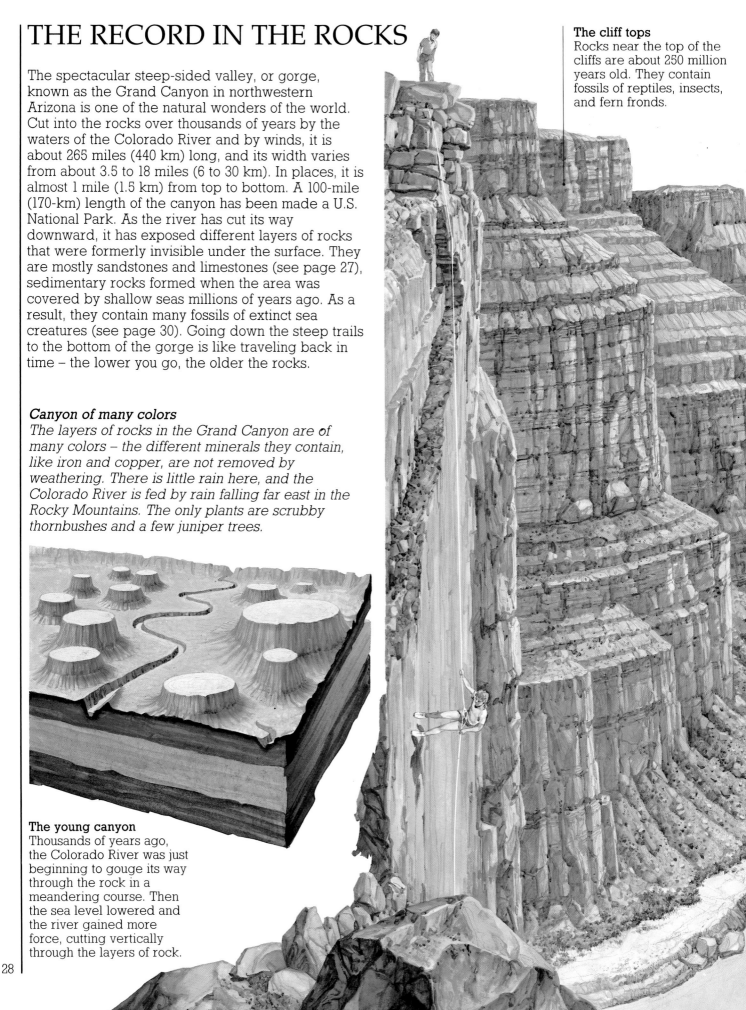

The young canyon
Thousands of years ago, the Colorado River was just beginning to gouge its way through the rock in a meandering course. Then the sea level lowered and the river gained more force, cutting vertically through the layers of rock.

The cliff tops
Rocks near the top of the cliffs are about 250 million years old. They contain fossils of reptiles, insects, and fern fronds.

The steep wall
Halfway down the canyon, the limestones are about 400 million years old. The fossils here include fish with bony plates of armor. Further down, the fish disappear and the only traces of life are wiggly lines – perhaps trails of worms or shellfish in the ancient seabed.

Rock pile
Near the bottom, the rocks are 2 billion years old; they contain no traces of animal or plant life. Heaped on them are piles of broken stones and debris along the riverbanks. Many of these have been broken off the walls above by the action of wind, rain, and ice.

River bed

The story of life

200 million years ago

400 million years ago

500 million years ago

The rock layers of the Grand Canyon are still flat and horizontal, roughly as they were laid down millions of years ago. Each layer contains a fossilized selection of the animals and plants alive when it was formed. The creatures above – found in the fossils – show the story of life in this area through the ages.

The riverbed
The Colorado River is still cutting downward, making the canyon ever deeper. Often the water is hidden by hanging mists. Sometimes the river floods and scours clean its banks.

PRESERVED IN STONE

Rocks can tell a fascinating story because they sometimes contain traces of once-living things that have been preserved as fossils – literally turned into stone. How did it happen? Many thousands of years ago, an animal or plant died and sank to the bottom of a lake, river, or sea. The soft parts of its body soon rotted away. But the hard parts, such as bones, teeth, or shells, remained and became covered as more sand or mud settled on top. Gradually, water seeped into the bone or shell, carrying minerals that turned it into stone. As the layers of mud and sand were squashed down, the remains got buried deeper and deeper, and the mud or sand eventually turned into the form of rock – known as sedimentary rock – in which the fossils were later found.

Fossils from rocks of different ages, many, many hundreds of years apart, can be used to build up a picture – the "fossil record" – of how life on Earth has changed. The very earliest fossils in rocks more than 3 billion years old are of microscopic, bloblike creatures. Exactly what made them is not known. Rocks from 590 million years ago contain fossils of familiar-looking shellfish and other creatures. About 240 million years ago, the fossils of the first dinosaurs appeared, but by 65 million years ago, they had disappeared, and fossils of mammals became more common.

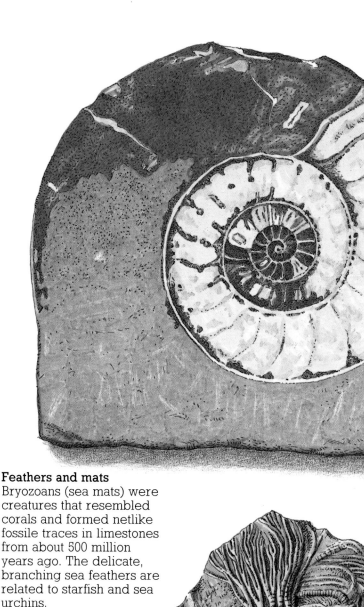

Back to the beginning of life
Fossilized remains of animals and plants from millions of years ago are shown here. Because of the way the rocks in which they are found are formed, the fossils found in the lower layers are usually older than those in the upper layers. In recent years, the age of some rock has been measured by detecting how much of a certain kind of radiation they contain. This radioactive dating *can determine the age of a rock within a few million years.*

Feathers and mats
Bryozoans (sea mats) were creatures that resembled corals and formed netlike fossile traces in limestones from about 500 million years ago. The delicate, branching sea feathers are related to starfish and sea urchins.

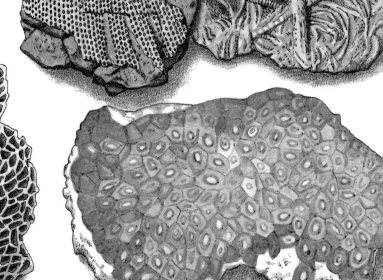

Corals
The tiny creatures called corals build cup-shaped limestone skeletons (see page 50) that form good fossils. Most reef-forming fossil corals date from about 230 million years ago.

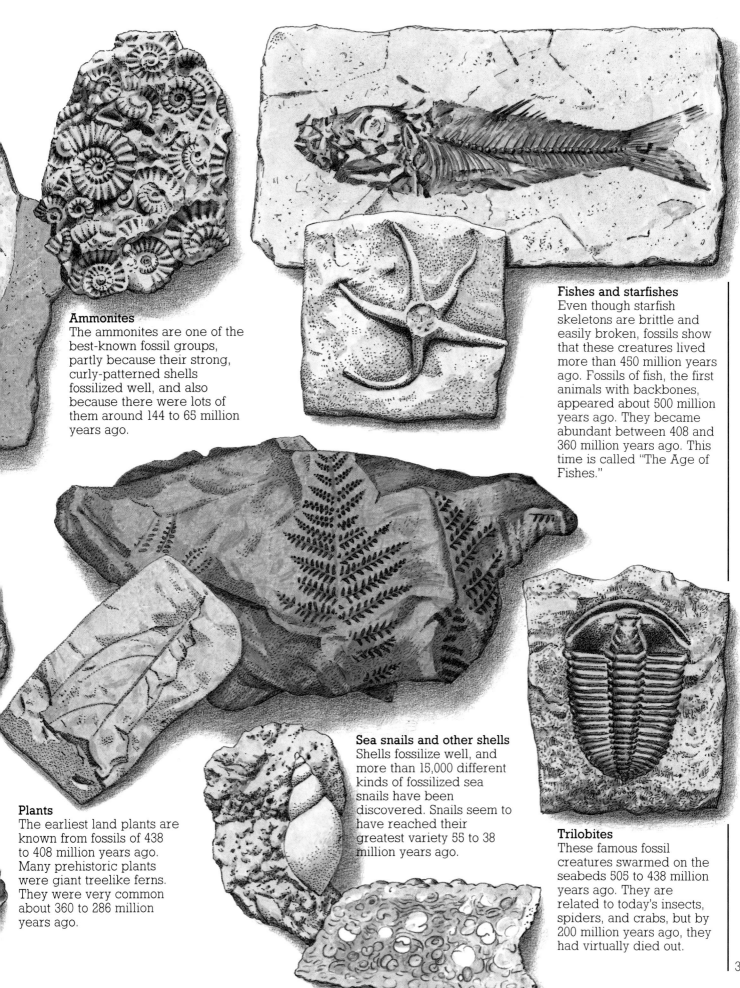

Ammonites

The ammonites are one of the best-known fossil groups, partly because their strong, curly-patterned shells fossilized well, and also because there were lots of them around 144 to 65 million years ago.

Fishes and starfishes

Even though starfish skeletons are brittle and easily broken, fossils show that these creatures lived more than 450 million years ago. Fossils of fish, the first animals with backbones, appeared about 500 million years ago. They became abundant between 408 and 360 million years ago. This time is called "The Age of Fishes."

Plants

The earliest land plants are known from fossils of 438 to 408 million years ago. Many prehistoric plants were giant treelike ferns. They were very common about 360 to 286 million years ago.

Sea snails and other shells

Shells fossilize well, and more than 15,000 different kinds of fossilized sea snails have been discovered. Snails seem to have reached their greatest variety 55 to 38 million years ago.

Trilobites

These famous fossil creatures swarmed on the seabeds 505 to 438 million years ago. They are related to today's insects, spiders, and crabs, but by 200 million years ago, they had virtually died out.

THE CHANGING WEATHER

What's the weather like today? Is it sunny, or cloudy, or rainy? Perhaps even foggy or snowy? Our weather is constantly changing, both from place to place and in the same place on different days. At this moment, there may be rain in Rome, sun in San Francisco, and clouds in Calcutta.

But it is very unlikely to be snowing in the Sahara or warm enough to sunbathe at the South Pole. Because, although the weather varies from day to day (and even from minute to minute), on a longer time scale it is more predictable. Different parts of the world have their own regular yearly weather patterns. We call the long-term pattern the *climate*.

What makes the weather change? The answer begins with the Sun. As the Earth spins around, the Sun's rays warm different parts of the atmosphere (see pages 8-11). Warmed air rises and pushes cooler air to one side. This moving air is wind. As air rises, it cools and its *water vapor* condenses to form clouds and rain (see page 34). The Sun also controls average temperatures. Tropical areas are warm because the Sun's rays come down from directly overhead. They have little atmosphere to pass through, and so not much of their heat is absorbed. At the poles, the sun's slanting rays pass through much more atmosphere. More of their heat is absorbed, and so at ground level the rays are not so warm.

Weather eye in the sky
About 600 miles (1,000 km) above the Earth, an orbiting satellite takes photographs of cloud banks and other weather features and beams them down as radio signals to a receiving station on the ground. Here, computers create the "satellite pictures" seen each day on TV. These satellites help weather experts make more accurate predictions.

Clear and sunny
Areas where there are no clouds must be having sunny weather! The Earth's surface is laid out like a giant map, with the mountains, lakes, and coastlines clearly visible. The cameras on board modern satellites can take photographs in amazing detail. They can even make out shapes as small as a car.

Rain on the way
The tops of clouds look different from the undersides that we see from Earth. These dark clouds (*nimbostratus*) are a sign that it is raining beneath. In some areas of the tropics it always rains heavily for certain weeks of the year, a time called the *monsoon* season.

Blowing in the wind
The spinning of the Earth tends to make winds bend to the right in the northern half of the world and to the left in the southern half. This is called the Coriolis effect. In some ocean areas near the equator, there may be no wind for weeks.

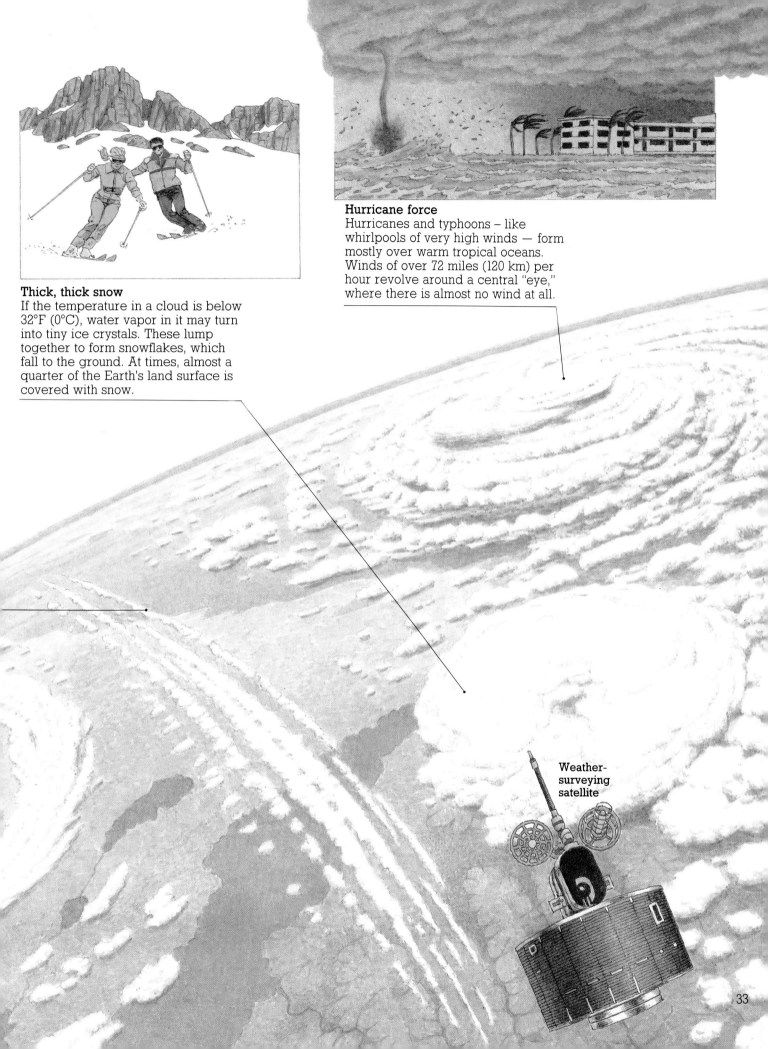

Thick, thick snow
If the temperature in a cloud is below 32°F (0°C), water vapor in it may turn into tiny ice crystals. These lump together to form snowflakes, which fall to the ground. At times, almost a quarter of the Earth's land surface is covered with snow.

Hurricane force
Hurricanes and typhoons – like whirlpools of very high winds — form mostly over warm tropical oceans. Winds of over 72 miles (120 km) per hour revolve around a central "eye," where there is almost no wind at all.

Weather-surveying satellite

WATER GOES AROUND AND AROUND

Water is everywhere, but not always visible. Did you know that it covers seven-tenths of the Earth's surface as seas and oceans, and that two-thirds of your body is made up of water? The quantity of water on Earth is always the same, but the water itself moves around. The Sun's rays warm it, and it apparently "dries," but it, in fact, turns into invisible water vapor that passes into the atmosphere in a process called evaporation. As the water vapor rises upward, the air becomes cooler, and the water vapor turns back (*condenses*) into billions of tiny water droplets so light that they do not fall. Masses of these droplets form clouds. From time to time, the droplets join together to make one drop of water. Too heavy to float, it falls to Earth as a raindrop.

This sequence is called the water cycle, and it is part of our weather. Clouds and rain, ice and snow are more common in some places than others. They have a great effect on what lives where, as you can find out on page 36.

Up in the clouds

Different types of clouds form at different heights, and each brings a certain kind of weather. Low, dark nimbostratus clouds mean rain. Huge, towering cumulonimbus clouds may bring thunderstorms. Some high mountains, like Everest, are often shrouded in clouds.

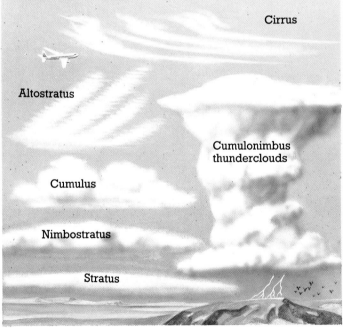

Cirrus

Altostratus

Cumulonimbus thunderclouds

Cumulus

Nimbostratus

Stratus

Water on the move

The Earth's water goes around unceasingly. Snow and rain fall to the ground and run as glaciers and rivers to the sea. Water from the land, sea, plants, and animals passes back into the atmosphere as water vapor. You are part of this cycle. Your steamy breath on a cold morning is the vapor from your lungs condensing into water droplets.

1 Snow falling

In cold areas and over mountains, and in winter, the water often returns to the Earth's surface as snow. Eventually the Sun's rays melt the snow. Then the water runs into gutters, gulleys, and streams and back into the ocean.

Snow falls on high ground

Glaciers melt into ocean

Evaporation from glaciers

2 Evaporation

Even on a cold day, the Sun's rays and the drying effect of wind encourage water to turn from liquid into water vapor in the air (*evaporate*). Water evaporates from rivers, lakes, glaciers, snowfields, and city streets!

3 Rain, rain, go away

Rain occurs when moist winds from the sea blow over the land. Rain also comes from depressions (low-pressure air systems) and from thunderclouds that form on hot summer days.

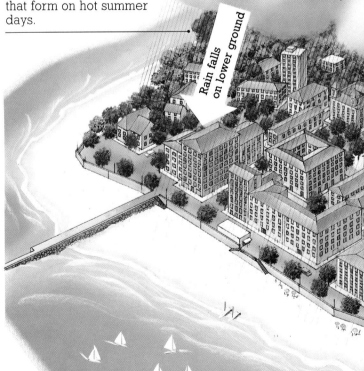

Rain falls on lower ground

34

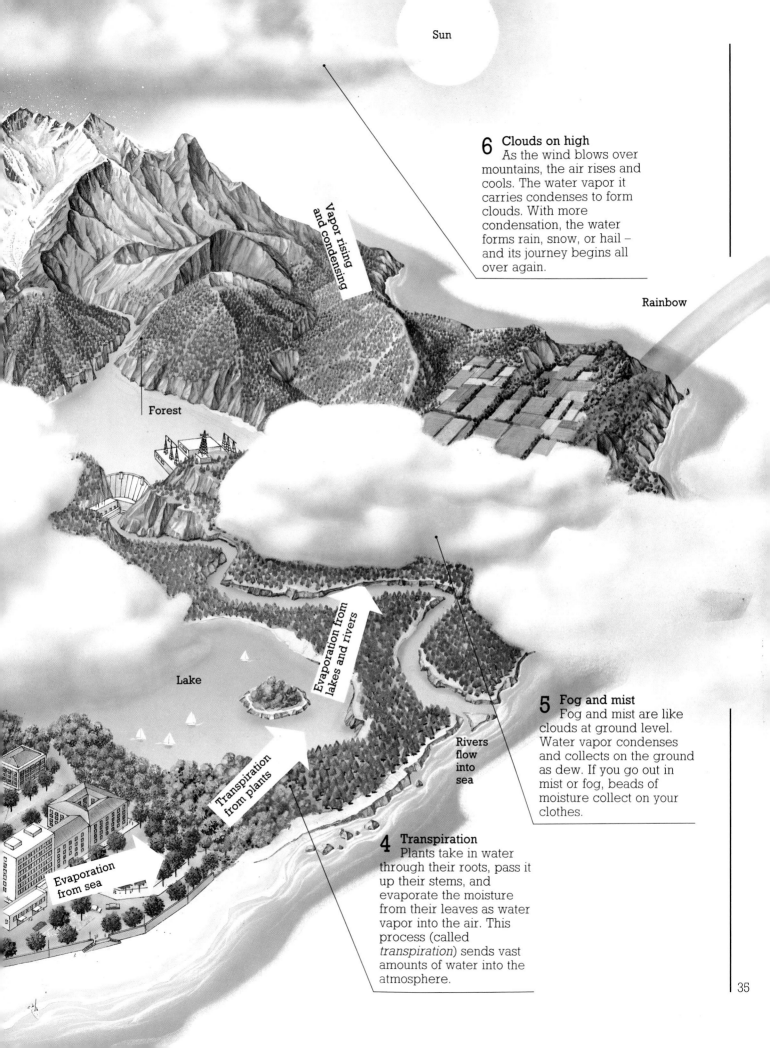

Sun

6 Clouds on high
As the wind blows over mountains, the air rises and cools. The water vapor it carries condenses to form clouds. With more condensation, the water forms rain, snow, or hail – and its journey begins all over again.

Rainbow

Vapor rising and condensing

Forest

Lake

Evaporation from lakes and rivers

Transpiration from plants

Evaporation from sea

Rivers flow into sea

5 Fog and mist
Fog and mist are like clouds at ground level. Water vapor condenses and collects on the ground as dew. If you go out in mist or fog, beads of moisture collect on your clothes.

4 Transpiration
Plants take in water through their roots, pass it up their stems, and evaporate the moisture from their leaves as water vapor into the air. This process (called *transpiration*) sends vast amounts of water into the atmosphere.

LIFE AROUND THE WORLD

Plants and animals live in nearly all parts of the world, but the wildlife at the icy poles is completely different from that at the steamy, hot equator. Temperature and water are the keys to what lives where. The hotter and damper it is, within reason, the more plants and creatures there are, and the greater the variety. But many of the plants and animals around the world have adapted over millions of years to cope with very difficult conditions – polar animals have extra layers of fat to cope with the cold, for example.

As you travel north or south from the equator, the average temperature gradually falls because the Sun's rays are weakened by passing through more atmosphere (see page 32). At the equator, the temperature is about 77° to 86°F (25° to 30°C) every day. Near the South Pole, it may rise above freezing in midsummer, but the average is -58°F (-50°C) – far colder than your freezer. These "bands" of temperature around the Earth create different types of plant and animal life suited to the particular conditions. Because ocean currents and winds affect temperature, and because rainfall varies, the bands are not identical on both sides of the equator.

Each region has its own climate (see page 32) and particular animals that have adapted to it.

What grows where
An imaginary view from pole to equator (continued on page 38-39) shows that the rising temperatures closer to the equator bring with them a greater variety of plants and animals. Each region is usually named after the plants that grow in greatest abundance, such as coniferous trees or grassland. This is because the plants that grow determine the type of animals that have adapted best to living there.

Snowline

Treeline

Iceberg

Polar bears

Seals

Pack ice

Penguins

Hardwood, broad-leaved trees:
beech, oak, elm

Magpie

Alpine tundra

Coniferous
trees

Grizzly bear

Fallow
deer

Reindeer

Badger

Fox

Moose

Mossy tundra

Lynx

Temperate forest
The term "temperate"
describes the cool region of
the world. In its forests, trees
such as oaks and maples lose
their leaves in winter. Badgers,
foxes, martens, squirrels, and
various types of deer live in
these woodlands.

Coniferous forest
South of the tundra are vast
tracts of evergreen, cone-
bearing trees called conifers,
whose needle-shaped leaves
withstand the freezing winters.

Tundra
Around the frozen Arctic are
the treeless lands called
tundra. They are ice-covered
in winter, but during the brief
summer, mosses and flowers
spring up, providing food for
reindeer, lemmings, and other
creatures.

Polar ice cap
At the ends of the Earth, life-giving
fresh water is frozen solid. So there
are no land plants. Only the surface of
the sea freezes. Underneath are tiny
floating plankton or fish, providing
food for a few large creatures that can
live in or near the water. These
include polar bears (from the Arctic)
and penguins (from the Antarctic).

Grassland

Desert

Polar ice cap

Coniferous
forest

Tropical forest

Temperate
forest

Tundra

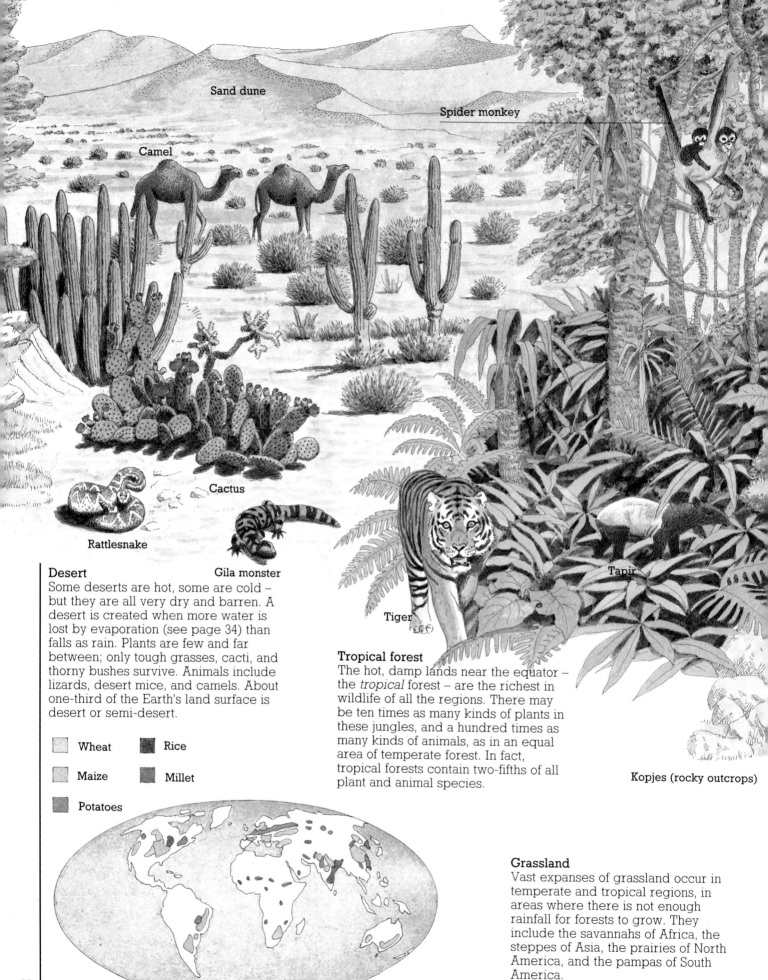

Sand dune

Spider monkey

Camel

Cactus

Rattlesnake

Gila monster

Desert

Some deserts are hot, some are cold –
but they are all very dry and barren. A
desert is created when more water is
lost by evaporation (see page 34) than
falls as rain. Plants are few and far
between; only tough grasses, cacti, and
thorny bushes survive. Animals include
lizards, desert mice, and camels. About
one-third of the Earth's land surface is
desert or semi-desert.

☐ Wheat ■ Rice

☐ Maize ■ Millet

■ Potatoes

Tiger

Tapir

Tropical forest

The hot, damp lands near the equator –
the *tropical* forest – are the richest in
wildlife of all the regions. There may
be ten times as many kinds of plants in
these jungles, and a hundred times as
many kinds of animals, as in an equal
area of temperate forest. In fact,
tropical forests contain two-fifths of all
plant and animal species.

Kopjes (rocky outcrops)

Grassland

Vast expanses of grassland occur in
temperate and tropical regions, in
areas where there is not enough
rainfall for forests to grow. They
include the savannahs of Africa, the
steppes of Asia, the prairies of North
America, and the pampas of South
America.

Toucan

Hornbill

Gibbon

Lianas and vines

Nature under the plow

If you compare our planet today with how it was 5,000 years ago, you will find there have been enormous changes. Vast tracts of land that were once "wild" have been turned over to farming or industry. The prairies of North America are still grasslands, but the original wild grasses (and the buffalo that grazed them) have all but disappeared. Today, these soils are plowed and sown with wheat and other food crops. The temperate forests that once covered much of Europe have been cut down for timber to build ships, houses, and furniture. In their place are fields of rice, barley, beets, potatoes, and other food crops. The tropical forests, nature's richest storehouses, are being cut down for hardwood timber, for industries like papermaking, and to make way for farmlands and factories at the rate of an area the size of New York City every four days.

Giraffe

Acacia tree

Zebra

Wildebeest

Rhinoceros

Lion

MAKING NEW LAND

Throughout the history of the Earth, there has been an endless battle between the land and the sea. It is still happening today. In some parts of the world, the sea is winning and the coastline is being eaten away (see page 48). But in other areas, as in the Mississippi Delta, shown here, land has the upper hand. Why is this?

As a river enters the sea, its waters flow less quickly. The tiny waterborne particles of sand, silt, mud, and clay begin to sink and then slowly settle. Sand and other relatively large particles settle first, near the shore. The smallest particles, such as clays, may be carried many miles out to sea before they sink. This settling out is called *sedimentation* and the particles *sediments*. As they collect, they raise the seabed. In certain conditions (see below) a strip of land forms around the river's mouth and advances into the sea, as more sediments add to it. This is a river *delta*, and it is land won from the sea. It has happened, for example, in Egypt at the mouth of the Nile, in India at the mouth of the Ganges, and here at the mouth of the Mississippi. It can happen fast, too: the Mississippi Delta is growing by about 295 feet (90 m) each year!

How a delta forms

Some deltas are delicate – the loose sediments can be washed away in a single storm. But coastal plants, such as mangrove trees and marram grass on sand dunes, help to make them more permanent. The plants grow into the shallow water, slowing down the flow of water, so more particles settle. Over hundreds of years, the loose sediments turn into firm, dry land. Eventually, they become sedimentary rock (see page 26).

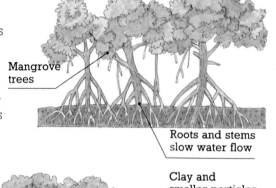

Mangrove trees

Roots and stems slow water flow

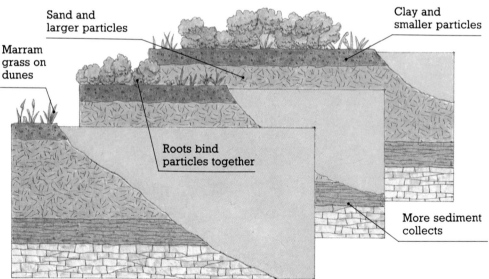

Marram grass on dunes

Sand and larger particles

Clay and smaller particles

Roots bind particles together

More sediment collects

"Ol' Man River" and his delta

The great Mississippi River collects water from two-fifths of the U.S. land area and flows into the Gulf of Mexico near New Orleans. (Its name comes from an Algonquin Indian word for "Father of Waters.") Over hundreds of years, shifts in the river's course, as one channel silts up, have altered the position of the delta. In this aerial view, taken by satellite, the red areas show the land.

The Mississippi Delta 3,000 years ago

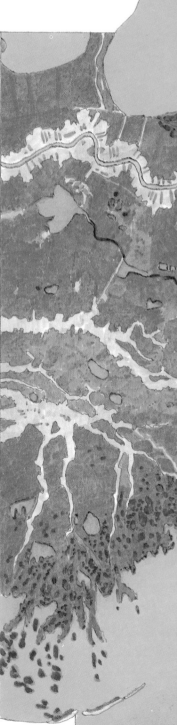

Satellite

Where the delta was
About 3,000 years ago, these islands marked the edge of the delta. But the ocean's waves and currents gradually wore away the middle part of the delta, and only a chain of barrier islands now remains.

The river today
Each year, the Mississippi pours more than 500 million tons of sand, mud, and other sediments into the Gulf of Mexico. Some of these particles have traveled over 2,100 miles (3,500 km) from the river's source far inland to the north.

The delta of the future?
Winds and ocean currents sweep the sediments southward from the river's mouth, clouding the water for many miles. In thousands of years, this area may become dry land, and the river will have moved on.

NATURE'S SCULPTURES

Rocks may seem hard and unbreakable to us. But even "solid rock" is no match for the forces of nature. Wind picks up sand grains and other particles and hurls them against a rock, sandblasting grooves and cracks in its surface. The Sun beats down by day, making the rock expand; during chilly nights, the rock cools and shrinks. This makes a thousand tiny cracks in its surface.

Rain beats down, getting into the grooves and cracks and weakening the rock. Floodwaters and rivers scour its surface. The chemicals that water absorbs from the air and soil turn it into a very weak acid, which slowly dissolves away certain types of rock, such as limestone.

When water freezes into ice, it expands with considerable force. Water freezing in the grooves and cracks of the rock splits and splinters it. And those rivers of ice, glaciers (see page 46), carve away great valleys. All these forces of erosion wear down even the hardest rocks.

Shaped in stone
Striking rock formations around the Earth (but shown here together) have been carved by the forces of erosion. Some types of rocks are much harder and more resistant than others. As the softer, weaker rocks around them are worn away, the tougher rocks remain as weird and wonderful shapes – nature's sculptures.

Elephants in the desert
In the Sahara Desert, sandstones 420 million years old have been cracked and chipped by erosion into the huge cliffs of Tassili n'Ajjer. Cave paintings 7,000 years old depict elephants and antelopes, showing that grass and trees covered the area at that time.

Giant's pebbles
The Harz Mountains, in central Germany, were once granite rocks far below the surface. Many cycles of erosion and uplifting have brought them to the surface. Boulders as big as houses lie jumbled like pebbles dropped by a giant.

Valle de la Luna
In northern Argentina, in the foothills of the Andes, is the dry, desolate "Valley of the Moon." Rock columns have been chiseled by windblown sand. Yet fossils in the area show it was once moist and inhabited by giant ferns, lizards, and snakes.

A tall old man
The Old Man of Hoy is a rock 452 feet (137 m) tall, in the sea near the Orkney Islands. Made of extra-hard sandstone, it was once part of a long cliff that was worn away by the sea.

Smoothed by rain
Heavy monsoon rains have helped to erode the Western Ghats, a mountain chain in western India. Here, a tough cap of rock is an "umbrella" to the rain-smoothed cone beneath.

The great bear
In northern Sardinia is a granite headland that has been eroded by – dew! Dew settles in the night and chemically attacks the rock, lingering longer in the shadier places before the Sun dries it. Flakes of rock are loosened and blown away, forming bowl-shaped hollows. This rock is called *Capo d'Orso*, the "Cape of the Bear." Can you see why?

City of stone
Ciudad Encantada, the "Enchanted City," is near Madrid in Spain. But these bizarre rocky outcrops are not the work of people. Over centuries, hard dolomite slabs have protected portions of the lower limestone from chemical erosion by rainwater (page 44), creating stone "skyscrapers."

43

THE WORLD UNDER OUR FEET

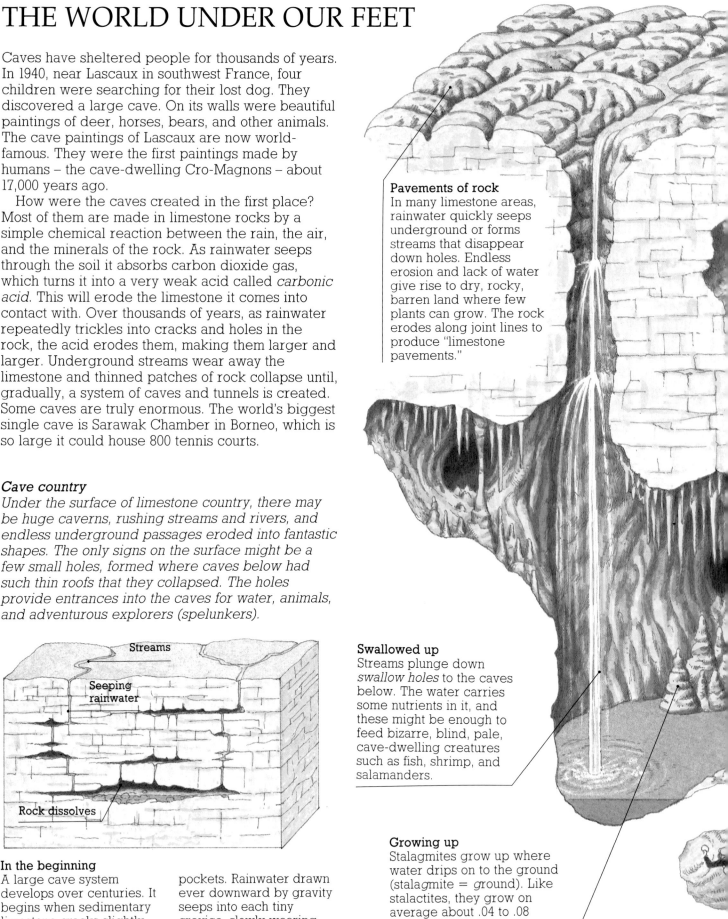

Caves have sheltered people for thousands of years. In 1940, near Lascaux in southwest France, four children were searching for their lost dog. They discovered a large cave. On its walls were beautiful paintings of deer, horses, bears, and other animals. The cave paintings of Lascaux are now world-famous. They were the first paintings made by humans – the cave-dwelling Cro-Magnons – about 17,000 years ago.

How were the caves created in the first place? Most of them are made in limestone rocks by a simple chemical reaction between the rain, the air, and the minerals of the rock. As rainwater seeps through the soil it absorbs carbon dioxide gas, which turns it into a very weak acid called *carbonic acid*. This will erode the limestone it comes into contact with. Over thousands of years, as rainwater repeatedly trickles into cracks and holes in the rock, the acid erodes them, making them larger and larger. Underground streams wear away the limestone and thinned patches of rock collapse until, gradually, a system of caves and tunnels is created. Some caves are truly enormous. The world's biggest single cave is Sarawak Chamber in Borneo, which is so large it could house 800 tennis courts.

Cave country
Under the surface of limestone country, there may be huge caverns, rushing streams and rivers, and endless underground passages eroded into fantastic shapes. The only signs on the surface might be a few small holes, formed where caves below had such thin roofs that they collapsed. The holes provide entrances into the caves for water, animals, and adventurous explorers (spelunkers).

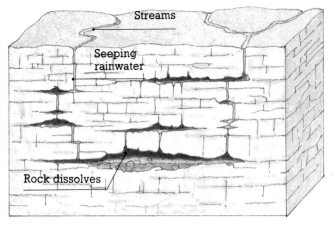

Streams

Seeping rainwater

Rock dissolves

In the beginning
A large cave system develops over centuries. It begins when sedimentary limestone cracks slightly during earth movements to form small cracks and pockets. Rainwater drawn ever downward by gravity seeps into each tiny crevice, slowly wearing away the rock and enlarging the crevices.

Pavements of rock
In many limestone areas, rainwater quickly seeps underground or forms streams that disappear down holes. Endless erosion and lack of water give rise to dry, rocky, barren land where few plants can grow. The rock erodes along joint lines to produce "limestone pavements."

Swallowed up
Streams plunge down *swallow holes* to the caves below. The water carries some nutrients in it, and these might be enough to feed bizarre, blind, pale, cave-dwelling creatures such as fish, shrimp, and salamanders.

Growing up
Stalagmites grow up where water drips on to the ground (stala*g*mite = *g*round). Like stalactites, they grow on average about .04 to .08 inches (1 to 2 mm) each year, to 26 feet (2 m) or more high.

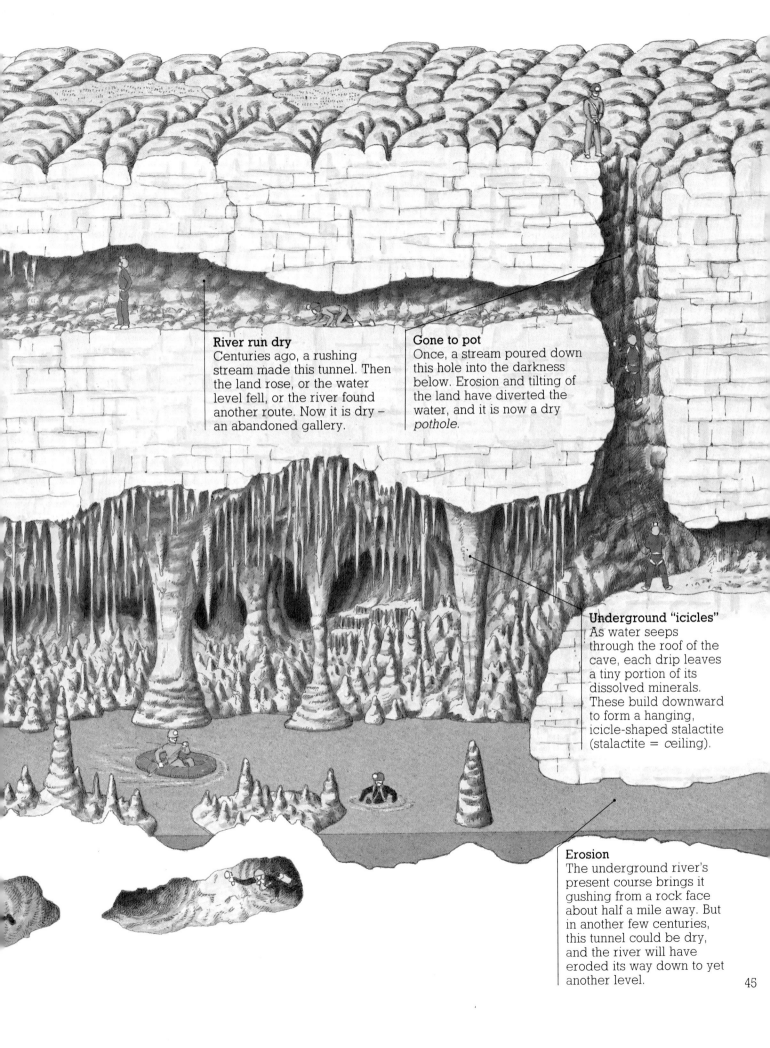

River run dry
Centuries ago, a rushing stream made this tunnel. Then the land rose, or the water level fell, or the river found another route. Now it is dry – an abandoned gallery.

Gone to pot
Once, a stream poured down this hole into the darkness below. Erosion and tilting of the land have diverted the water, and it is now a dry *pothole*.

Underground "icicles"
As water seeps through the roof of the cave, each drip leaves a tiny portion of its dissolved minerals. These build downward to form a hanging, icicle-shaped stalactite (stala*c*tite = *c*eiling).

Erosion
The underground river's present course brings it gushing from a rock face about half a mile away. But in another few centuries, this tunnel could be dry, and the river will have eroded its way down to yet another level.

45

THE FROZEN LANDSCAPE

Did you know that ice covers more than one-tenth of the Earth's land area? It is formed as snow falls and gets squashed under its own weight, or as it thaws and refreezes. Of course, ice only forms where temperatures are below freezing – the polar regions – or high up in the mountains. Almost the entire continent of Antarctica, at the South Pole, is under a blanket of ice one and a half times the size of the U.S. and over 13,200 feet (4,000 m) thick in places. Three-quarters of our planet's fresh water is locked up as ice covering the land.

Great snowfields in the highest mountains of the world feed thousands of massive glaciers, "rivers of ice," that flow very slowly downhill. The rocks frozen in the base and sides of a glacier can hollow out a mountainside, polish the rocks, and even transport underneath it immense boulders weighing hundreds of tons. In former times, the biggest glaciers carved away parts of our landscape, which are now warmer and ice-free, into giant valleys.

The hidden ice at sea
An iceberg is a huge block of freshwater ice that has floated off from the end of a glacier into a lake or the sea. It is much bigger than it looks – only about one-sixth of its bulk shows above the water's surface.

Block iceberg

Rounded iceberg

The massive "rivers of ice"
The bird's-eye view of a glacier shows how this vast conveyor belt of ice changes the landscape. A glacier slides along, on average, at about 3 feet (1.1 m) each day, but a few, especially in Canada, flow at 80 feet (25 m) or more per day. The longest glacier in the world, 240 miles (400 km) in length, is in Antarctica.

The glacier's snout
The lower end, or "snout," of the glacier may be on land, or in a lake or sea. Here it is a lot warmer, and the ice melts at the same rate as it flows downhill, forming a stream of icy water.

On the retreat
This glacier is getting smaller as it melts slightly faster than it is fed. Boulders made of rock, called *erratics*, carried down by the glacier indicate areas once covered by ice.

Big cracks in the ice
As the brittle ice flows around a sharp bend or over a ridge, it splits to form deep wedge-shaped cracks, called *crevasses*. Some are enormous – 165 feet (50 m) deep and hundreds of yards long.

The rubble on the sides
The moving ice rubs, rasps, and cracks the rock below, picking up bits of stone and boulders. These collect in mounds, known as *lateral moraines*, along the glacier's sides.

Yosemite Valley

Ice-sculpted landscapes
Millions of years ago, glaciers in many parts of the world wore away U-shaped valleys like the Yosemite Valley in California. Smaller valleys that open high on the sides of the main one are called *hanging valleys*. Ice may also gouge away the sides of a mountain to form a pointed peak and sharp ridges (*aretes*), as on Mount Fitzroy in Patagonia.

Mount Fitzroy

SEAS, TIDES, AND BEACHES

When most of us go to the seaside for our summer vacations, the skies are blue and the sea laps gently on the beach. But the same place in a winter's storm can look very different. The coastline becomes a battlegrond. Huge waves crash on the shore, hurling themselves against cliffs and rocks with colossal force and carrying away the broken fragments. Air does more damage than the water. Trapped by an incoming wave against the rock face, it is forced at high pressure into every nook and cranny of the rock, eventually cracking and splitting it. In many places, the sea relentlessly erodes the land, and ocean currents sweep away the debris. In other places, such as deltas (page 40), the land is winning. As the elements battle it out, the line between land and sea shifts and changes. Over the centuries, cliffs are eaten away, and sometimes whole villages and coastal towns are gradually swallowed up by the sea. Channels are blocked by fallen rocks, and sandbars form offshore. Maps and charts of coastal waters must be constantly updated so that sailors do not run their boats aground.

Undercut and overhang
Sea cliffs are the best places to see how certain rocks were formed in layers. Storms and high tides undercut the lower cliff, and eventually the overhang crashes down as a pile of rubble.

Rolled by ocean rollers
Waves relentlessly roll rocks and boulders to and fro on the shore. Gradually, they are broken and worn into smaller pebbles and, over hundreds of years, into tiny particles called sand.

Sorted by size
Here, wind and waves have swept small sand grains from this area. But they are not strong enough to move larger, heavier boulders and pebbles. This process is called *sorting*.

Refreshed twice daily
Hollows and holes in the rocks fill with sea water to make rockpools. The water is refreshed at every high tide, bringing in floating bits of food and an ever-changing assortment of plants and animals.

Sea shells on the seashore
Hard, limy shells of sea animals are washed up on the shore and slowly broken into fragments, forming shelly sand.

On the beach

The shore is a fascinating example of erosion in action. Most beach sand has been brought from inland by rivers and swept along the coast by water currents. Some comes from erosion of the cliffs behind. Quartz is the most common mineral in sand grains, made from eroded rocks like granite.

Erosion slowdown

To slow erosion, *groins* (breakwaters) are built into the sea. They break up waves, lessen sideways currents, and reduce windblown sand. They also shelter seaweeds, limpets, barnacles, and other types of seashore life.

Tied to the tide

Each day, the sea level rises and falls, then rises and falls again (due to the gravitational pull of the Moon and the Sun; see page 10). The average time between one high tide and the next is 12 hours 25 minutes. The difference in height can be over 36 feet (10 m).

Tide flowing (coming in)

Tide ebbing (going out)

At the back of the beach

Winds blow sand grains inland to form dunes. Most plants find it difficult to get a roothold in the shifting grains, but a few, such as marram grass, are able to bind the sand and gradually stabilize the dunes.

Ocean currents

The Earth's rotation, its temperature zones, and its wind patterns help to create giant ocean currents that circulate around the globe. These ocean currents affect climate. For example, the warm waters of the Caribbean flow to northern Europe, creating mild winters.

Wind
Current

THE LIVING ROCKS IN THE OCEANS

Which tiny animals have over thousands of years built rocks in the oceans so huge that they can be seen from the Moon? Corals have. Each coral is a tiny, anemone-like sea creature about a fraction of an inch across. As it grows, it builds a minute cup-shaped skeleton to protect the lower part of its jellylike body, into which it can draw its tentacles for safety. The skeleton is made of calcium carbonate minerals that the coral obtains from sea water. Thousands of corals grow packed side by side, and their skeletons join together. When they die, more corals grow on top of them. Over many years, the millions of skeletons combine with sand and other fragments of matter to form a limestone rock, called a coral reef. The world's largest coral reef is the Great Barrier Reef off the coast of Australia. It is over 1,200 miles (2,000 km) long.

The rich life of the reef

Most corals grow in the warm, shallow seas of the tropics, where the water temperature is about 73° to 80°F (23° to 27°C). Most of the reefs are in the Caribbean and in the Indo-Pacific oceans. The caves, cracks, and underhangs in the coral reef are rich feeding grounds for a dazzling variety of fishes, crabs, shellfish, and other kinds of sea life, including sharks. The corals themselves are equally dazzling – and come in a myriad of types and colors.

Where corals grow

Corals live in shallow, sunny water. They usually grow best on the windward, most exposed side of a reef. Here the crashing waves aerate the water and prevent mud from suffocating the coral.

Seaweeds and algae

Leeward side

Coral growing on windward side

Bubble coral

This type of coral grows in rounded, bubblelike shapes. Like other corals, the tiny coral creatures come out only at night. They wave their tentacles in the sea water, stinging and eating any microscopic floating plants and animals they can catch.

Brain coral

This coral has a wavy-surface shape that looks like the human brain – hence its name! In life, coral is covered with a shiny layer of living tissue that shimmers in many colors. After death, only the whitish skeleton remains.

Hard coral

The skeletons of hard corals build up into low, flattened lumps of limestone. But not all corals make reefs. Some grow alone, like tiny sea anemones, lying on the seabed or stuck to rocks.

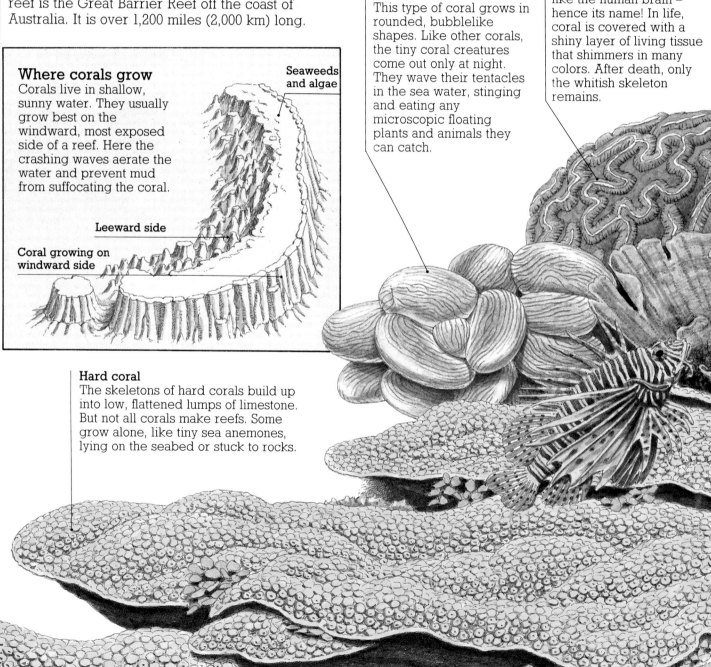

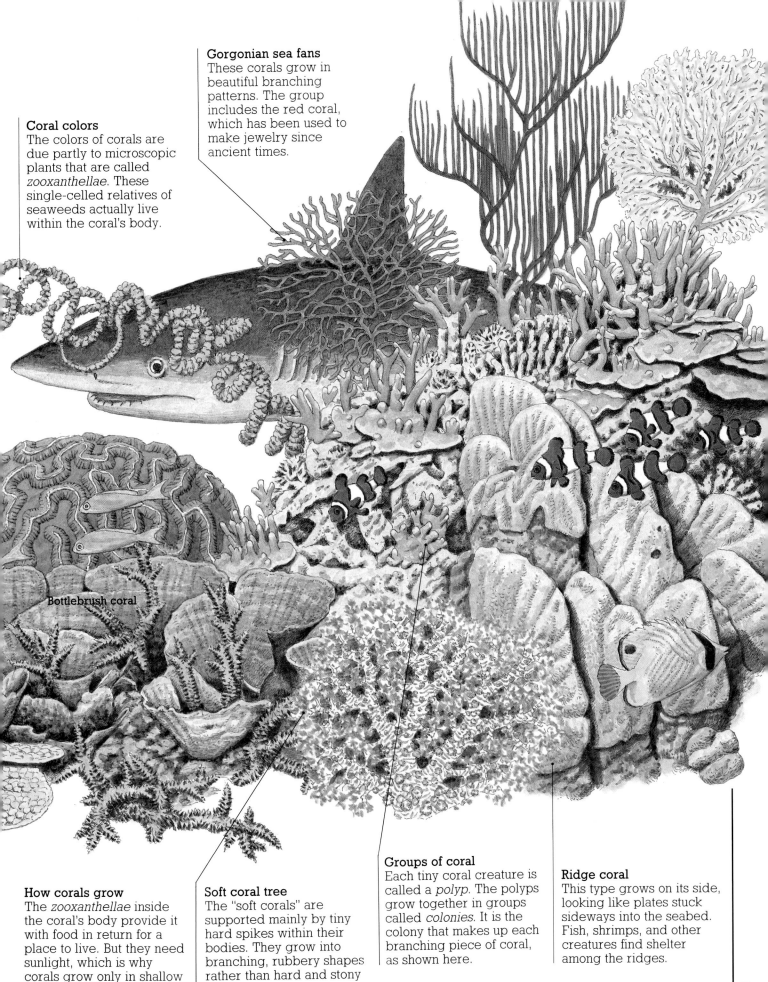

Coral colors
The colors of corals are due partly to microscopic plants that are called *zooxanthellae*. These single-celled relatives of seaweeds actually live within the coral's body.

Gorgonian sea fans
These corals grow in beautiful branching patterns. The group includes the red coral, which has been used to make jewelry since ancient times.

Bottlebrush coral

How corals grow
The *zooxanthellae* inside the coral's body provide it with food in return for a place to live. But they need sunlight, which is why corals grow only in shallow water.

Soft coral tree
The "soft corals" are supported mainly by tiny hard spikes within their bodies. They grow into branching, rubbery shapes rather than hard and stony ones.

Groups of coral
Each tiny coral creature is called a *polyp*. The polyps grow together in groups called *colonies*. It is the colony that makes up each branching piece of coral, as shown here.

Ridge coral
This type grows on its side, looking like plates stuck sideways into the seabed. Fish, shrimps, and other creatures find shelter among the ridges.

EARTH'S MYSTERIES

In olden times, an eclipse of the Sun (opposite) struck terror into hearts across the world. The ancient Chinese and Babylonians could predict the movements of the Sun and the phases of the Moon. Yet they had no idea how the Solar System operated (see pages 8-11). When the Moon passed between the Earth and the Sun, eclipsing its light and warmth briefly, the ancient peoples thought it was a sign of the wrath of their god.

Nowadays, science can explain many of the strange happenings on our planet. And we know that forces far away in space affect what happens here on Earth. For instance, the Northern and Southern Lights are vast, moving curtains of light in the night sky toward the poles. People wondered why the lights brightened every 27 days or so, and then faded. Satellites and telescopes have helped to explain. The lights are electrical discharges, like those in a fluorescent light. They are formed when gases high in the atmosphere are hit by the "solar wind" – high-speed particles shot out from *sunspots* on the Sun. The Sun spins every 27 days, and the particles shoot out from its sunspots like the light beam from a lighthouse's rotating mirror. They "shine" on Earth every 27 days and illuminate the fabulous display of the polar lights.

Worldwide wonders
These strange happenings from around the world puzzled people for centuries, but now they can be explained by modern scientific knowledge. Yet there are still many important natural phenomena for earth scientists to explore, such as how to predict weather patterns and earthquakes more accurately.

Forests of stone
These rocks in Arizona look like broken tree trunks. Indeed, 200 million years ago, they were trees. Over millions of years, they were buried under sediments and *petrified* – turned into stone fossils made of agate and opal.

Colored clouds
"Mother-of-pearl" clouds (iridescent like the inside of an oyster shell) form at heights of 18 miles (30 km) when temperatures are very cold – down to −112°F (−80°C). They are made from ice crystals and water droplets that split sunlight into its many different colors.

No nighttime
North of the Arctic Circle, the Sun, for at least one night in summer, does not disappear below the horizon. This is due to the tilt of the axis around which the Earth spins (see page 11). The closer you get to the North Pole, the more days there are with "Midnight Sun." At the pole itself, there are almost six months of daylight in summer, and six months of winter darkness. The same happens at the South Pole.

Now you see it . . .

A mirage is something that appears to be there but is only an image of something far away. Some mirages are formed because light, bent by warm air near the ground, reaches an observer many miles away – yet forms an image that seems nearby.

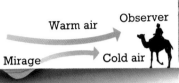

Solar eclipse

As the Moon goes around the Earth, and the Earth goes around the Sun, the Moon occasionally passes in front of the Sun and temporarily blots out the light (*eclipses*).

Curtains of lights

Every 27 days colors glow in the night skies near the poles. The base of the "curtain" is about 60 miles (100 km) high, and the top may be over 180 miles (300 km) in altitude. Their brightness varies from year to year.

Northern lights
(*Aurora borealis*)

Southern lights
(*Aurora australis*)

It's snowing in the desert!

Freak strong, cold winds high in the atmosphere can bring snow over usually hot deserts. The snow settles on the desert sands and plants. However, it soon melts and soaks in or is dried out by the Sun.

Big Moon, small Moon

Photographs show that the Moon is "bigger" at some times of the month. This is because the orbit of the Moon around the Earth is not a circle, but an *ellipse*. When the Moon is closer to us, it looks larger than usual in the sky.

NATURAL RESOURCES

From the Earth's crust come the natural resources on which our modern world depends. Oil (petroleum), coal, and natural gas provide energy. Metals such as iron (for steel) and aluminum are used to make planes, trains, and road vehicles, and for machines of all kinds. Sand, stone, and clay make our buildings. We use lots of other natural substances, from the sulfur that hardens rubber for car tires to the silicon made into computer chips.

Of all the Earth's resources, oil is probably the most widely used and the most valuable. It has

formed from the bodies of tiny floating plants and animals that settled on the seabed over millions of years. Oil straight from the well is thick, dark, and gooey, known as "crude." But after separation into its various constituents at a *refinery*, it is used to make an almost endless list of substances: fuel in the form of gasoline, diesel fuel, and kerosene (for planes); oil for power stations; lubricating oils; waxes and solvents; and even hard materials – synthetic fibers, detergents, plastics of all kinds – as well as the inks on this page!

Drilling rig
The oil in a newly drilled well usually comes to the surface under natural pressure. Later, it has to be pumped up. The massive drill comes in sections and is hoisted by a crane into its housing, called a *derrick*.

A fortune under the seabed
Oil is found under the land and the ocean in sedimentary rocks that were once part of the seabed (see page 26). There are around 700 oil rigs dotted about the Earth's oceans. Some are test drilling to discover new oil and gas fields. Others, the production rigs, extract the oil and gas and feed it to the shore by pipeline or tanker.

Helipad

Lots of bores
A drilling rig bores up to a dozen holes into the oil "bubble" deep below. This helps to equalize the pressure in different parts of the oilfield and gives a more even flow.

Manifold

Oil production
Oil is inflammable, and drilling for it is risky. A *manifold* on the seabed controls the pressure and stops oil from spurting into the sea. A *flare stack* burns off the surplus gases in the oil. The crew live and work on the production platform, and the workers and supplies are ferried in and out by helicopter.

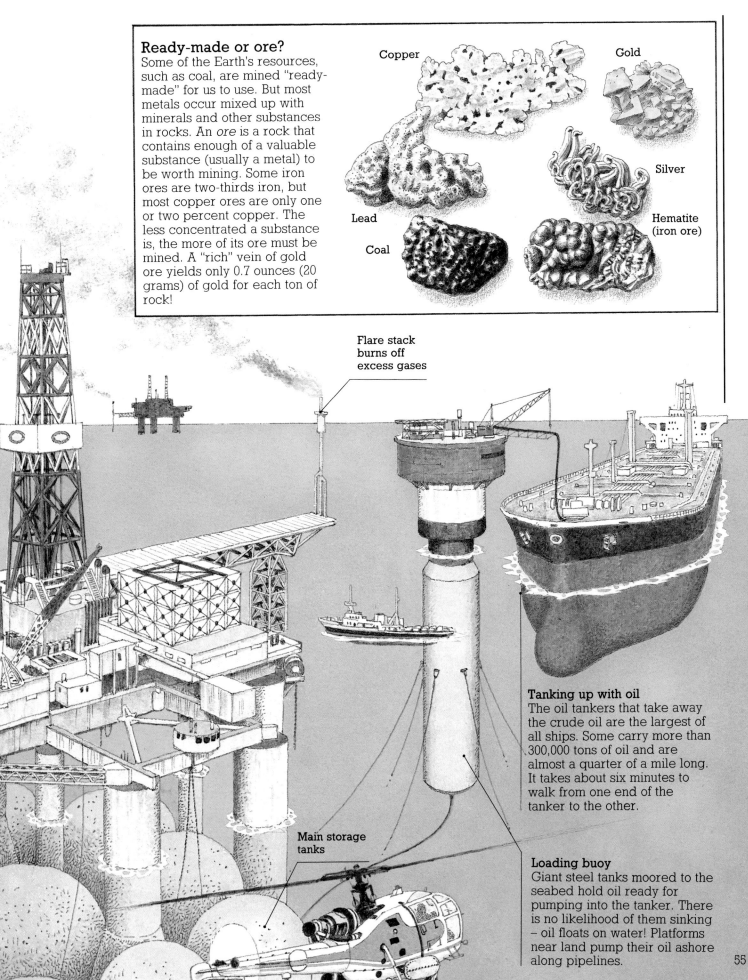

Ready-made or ore?
Some of the Earth's resources, such as coal, are mined "ready-made" for us to use. But most metals occur mixed up with minerals and other substances in rocks. An *ore* is a rock that contains enough of a valuable substance (usually a metal) to be worth mining. Some iron ores are two-thirds iron, but most copper ores are only one or two percent copper. The less concentrated a substance is, the more of its ore must be mined. A "rich" vein of gold ore yields only 0.7 ounces (20 grams) of gold for each ton of rock!

Copper

Gold

Lead

Silver

Coal

Hematite (iron ore)

Flare stack burns off excess gases

Main storage tanks

Tanking up with oil
The oil tankers that take away the crude oil are the largest of all ships. Some carry more than 300,000 tons of oil and are almost a quarter of a mile long. It takes about six minutes to walk from one end of the tanker to the other.

Loading buoy
Giant steel tanks moored to the seabed hold oil ready for pumping into the tanker. There is no likelihood of them sinking – oil floats on water! Platforms near land pump their oil ashore along pipelines.

55

EARTH'S TREASURE CHEST

"Beauty is in the eye of the beholder." If enough beholders think that something is beautiful, and it is in short supply, then it tends to be valuable as well. Gemstones are naturally occurring minerals that are valuable because of their natural beauty, durability, and rarity, and the way they are cut and polished (see below). Each gemstone has a characteristic pattern of cuts to produce tiny flat faces, called *facets*. Each facet is at a slight angle to the others so that light is reflected again and again to give each gem its characteristic sparkle.

There are about 3,000 different kinds of minerals in the Earth's crust. Only a hundred or so have exciting colors, patterning, and sparkle and could be called gemstones. Of these, only 15 or 20 are commonly used for jewelry, ornaments, and sculptures. The first stage is to mine the gem-containing rock. Most gems are rare, and many tons of rock must be sorted to obtain gems worth keeping. In a diamond mine, 25 tons of rock yield .035 ounces (1 gram) of diamonds, and most of these are almost too small to see. The second stage is cutting and polishing the gem from its rough, natural state so that its color, sheen, and sparkle are shown to best effect. Some gemstones are valuable for practical purposes as well. Diamonds and garnets are so hard that they are used in industry as cutting tools.

A priceless collection

Most of the gems shown here have been formed in the Earth over millions of years by the same enormous pressures and temperatures that have created the rocks around them. However, pearls, amber, ivory, and other substances formed by living things are technically not gems.

Amber (left)
The ancient Greeks thought that amber was the hardened rays of a sunset. In fact it is fossilized sap, or resin, from coniferous trees that grew millions of years ago.

Insect trapped in amber

Agate (above)
This is a form of quartz. It is created when gas bubbles trapped in molten rock slowly fill with layers of quartz colored by traces of iron and other elements.

Tourmaline (above)
Tourmaline, the birthstone for October, forms as slender crystals with three, six, or nine sides. It may be almost any color, from colorless to glossy black.

Jade (above)
Polished jade has a glassy look and a warm color, usually mottled green. It has been carved since ancient times by many peoples, especially the Chinese, into sculptures, ornaments, knives, and other tools.

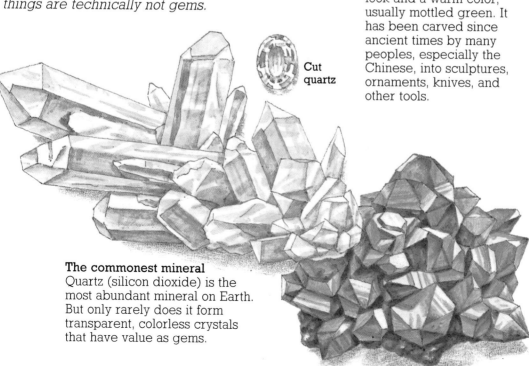

Cut quartz

The commonest mineral
Quartz (silicon dioxide) is the most abundant mineral on Earth. But only rarely does it form transparent, colorless crystals that have value as gems.

Turquoise (above)
Opaque rather than clear, and a beautiful brilliant blue or blue-green in color, these stones are usually cut and polished into rounded egg shapes.

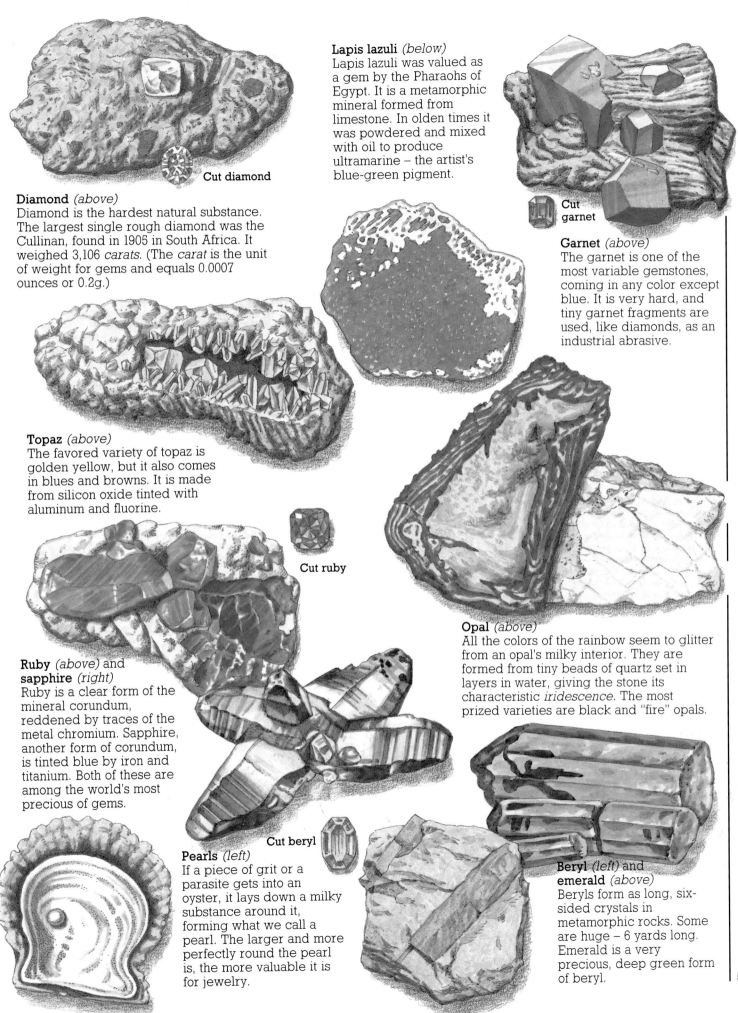

Lapis lazuli (below)
Lapis lazuli was valued as a gem by the Pharaohs of Egypt. It is a metamorphic mineral formed from limestone. In olden times it was powdered and mixed with oil to produce ultramarine – the artist's blue-green pigment.

Cut diamond

Diamond (above)
Diamond is the hardest natural substance. The largest single rough diamond was the Cullinan, found in 1905 in South Africa. It weighed 3,106 *carats*. (The *carat* is the unit of weight for gems and equals 0.0007 ounces or 0.2g.)

Cut garnet

Garnet (above)
The garnet is one of the most variable gemstones, coming in any color except blue. It is very hard, and tiny garnet fragments are used, like diamonds, as an industrial abrasive.

Topaz (above)
The favored variety of topaz is golden yellow, but it also comes in blues and browns. It is made from silicon oxide tinted with aluminum and fluorine.

Cut ruby

Opal (above)
All the colors of the rainbow seem to glitter from an opal's milky interior. They are formed from tiny beads of quartz set in layers in water, giving the stone its characteristic *iridescence*. The most prized varieties are black and "fire" opals.

Ruby (above) and **sapphire** (right)
Ruby is a clear form of the mineral corundum, reddened by traces of the metal chromium. Sapphire, another form of corundum, is tinted blue by iron and titanium. Both of these are among the world's most precious of gems.

Cut beryl

Pearls (left)
If a piece of grit or a parasite gets into an oyster, it lays down a milky substance around it, forming what we call a pearl. The larger and more perfectly round the pearl is, the more valuable it is for jewelry.

Beryl (left) and **emerald** (above)
Beryls form as long, six-sided crystals in metamorphic rocks. Some are huge – 6 yards long. Emerald is a very precious, deep green form of beryl.

57

POLLUTION OF THE PLANET

In today's overcrowded world, more and more of the Earth's natural resources are being used up. Although steps are being taken to control many forms of pollution, scientists and conservationists are particularly worried about these problems:

Acid rain (see below) The great pine forests of northern Europe and northern Canada are decaying and dying from the effects of acid rain, originating in industrial regions hundreds of miles away.

The greenhouse effect Burning gasoline, coal, forests or anything else creates the gas carbon dioxide. Its amounts are slowly building up, and scientists predict that the extra carbon dioxide will trap the Sun's warmth in the atmosphere, in the same way that glass traps warmth in a greenhouse. Gradually, the Earth's temperature will rise, with disastrous effects on climate, wildlife, and crops.

Radioactive pollution Nuclear power stations make cheap electricity and save valuable natural fuels, but the problem is how to dispose of the radioactive waste without future hazard.

The cost for the Earth
Each town has its factories, power stations, garbage dumps, and sewage plants. They are part of modern life, giving us the lifestyle and luxuries we take for granted. But there are many thousands of such towns around the Earth. How long can our planet cope with the pollution they produce?

Oil all gone
Fuel made from oil (petroleum), which took millions of years to form, will be guzzled up in a century at the present rate of use. Exhaust fumes from cars and trucks contain chemicals that help to create acid rain (right) and, in sunlight, make suffocating smog.

What goes up . . .
Fumes from vehicles, power stations, and factories dissolve in the water droplets of clouds, forming sulfuric acid. This falls back to Earth, perhaps hundreds of miles away, as *acid rain* which kills trees, fish, and wildlife.

Scarring the landscape
Where coal, metal ores, gemstones, gravel, building stones, and other valuable substances occur near the surface, great quarries and *open-cast* mines are dug to extract them. Fortunately, these days, most areas are re-landscaped by the mining and quarrying companies.

Blowing in the wind
Fertilizers, weedkillers, and pesticides are used by farmers to produce bigger yields from the crops. But the chemicals affect other plants, and animals as well, by seeping into the ground and polluting rivers and streams.

Undisposable disposables
Our modern society throws away endless "disposable" packages, containers, old furniture, beds, cars, machinery . . . Some of this will rot away when buried, but plastics, especially, do not. They pile up and will pollute the planet for hundreds of years to come unless a means of dissolving them is found.

Oil on troubled waters
Supertankers carry thousands of tons of oil from the oil fields to the industrial countries that use it. Accidental leaks and spillages are bound to occur, and oil slicks kill seabirds and marine life.

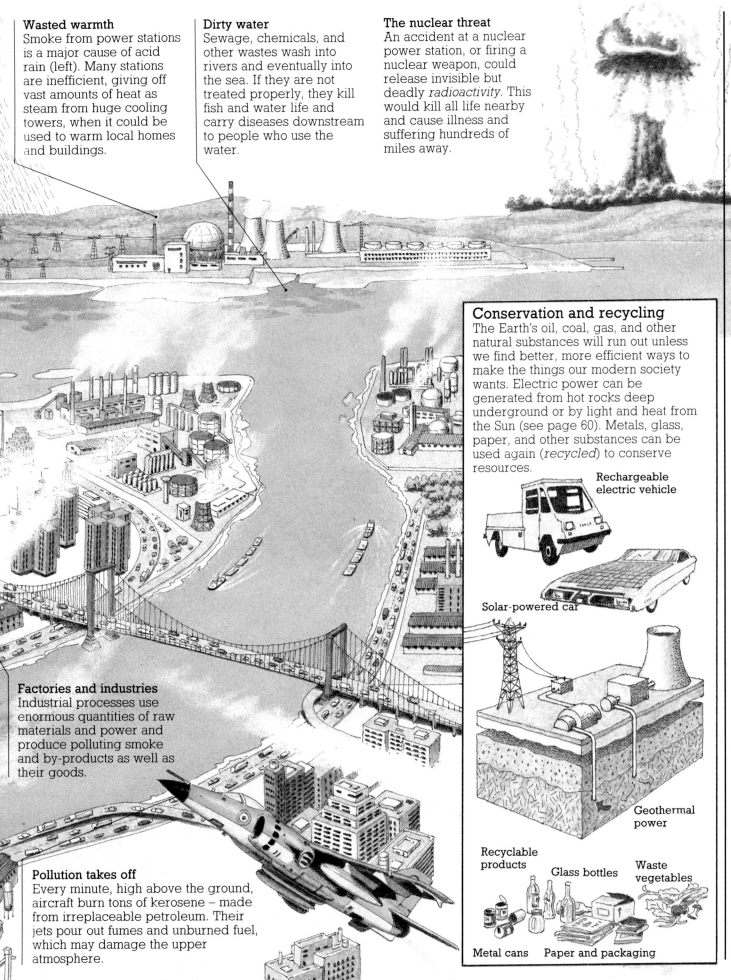

Wasted warmth
Smoke from power stations is a major cause of acid rain (left). Many stations are inefficient, giving off vast amounts of heat as steam from huge cooling towers, when it could be used to warm local homes and buildings.

Dirty water
Sewage, chemicals, and other wastes wash into rivers and eventually into the sea. If they are not treated properly, they kill fish and water life and carry diseases downstream to people who use the water.

The nuclear threat
An accident at a nuclear power station, or firing a nuclear weapon, could release invisible but deadly *radioactivity*. This would kill all life nearby and cause illness and suffering hundreds of miles away.

Conservation and recycling
The Earth's oil, coal, gas, and other natural substances will run out unless we find better, more efficient ways to make the things our modern society wants. Electric power can be generated from hot rocks deep underground or by light and heat from the Sun (see page 60). Metals, glass, paper, and other substances can be used again (*recycled*) to conserve resources.

Rechargeable electric vehicle

Solar-powered car

Geothermal power

Factories and industries
Industrial processes use enormous quantities of raw materials and power and produce polluting smoke and by-products as well as their goods.

Pollution takes off
Every minute, high above the ground, aircraft burn tons of kerosene – made from irreplaceable petroleum. Their jets pour out fumes and unburned fuel, which may damage the upper atmosphere.

Recyclable products

Glass bottles

Waste vegetables

Metal cans

Paper and packaging

59

NATURAL POWER

Our major energy sources today – coal, oil, natural gas – will not last for ever. The search is on for alternative forms of energy that are less polluting and that will last as long as the Earth itself. Hydro-electric dams, which harness the energy of moving water, are already in use in many countries. Harnessing tidal power is another possibility. A tidal power station on the Rance River in northern France generates 240 megawatts of electricity, enough to supply a small town. In fact, most natural power schemes are designed to turn their energy source into electricity. This is because electricity can be carried by cables, conveniently, silently, and without pollution, to wherever it is needed. Other forms of natural power – the tides, the wind, the Sun, for example – are only suitable for places with high tides, or strong, consistent winds, or plenty of sunshine. But covering a beautiful hillside with *solar cells* or windmills does tend to mar the landscape, and the whirring windmill blades create "noise pollution."

The ultimate energy source
The power-producing devices shown here each depend, in the end, on the Sun. Some use its light or heat directly. Others rely on winds, which are air movements caused by the Sun warming different parts of the atmosphere as the Earth rotates. Even falling water is sun-powered, since the Sun evaporated it from the sea to form clouds and fall as rain.

Falling water
A waterwheel turns because gravity pulls water downward over it. Old waterwheels turned millstones or pumped water to irrigate crops. Today, rushing water spins turbine blades that generate electricity in the hydroelectric power station.

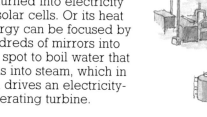

Circling sails
Windmills, a familiar sight two or three centuries ago, are used for various jobs, such as grinding wheat to make flour. Then power from coal and oil replaced the wind, and many windmills fell into disuse and disrepair.

Solar power
The Sun's light energy can be turned into electricity by solar cells. Or its heat energy can be focused by hundreds of mirrors into one spot to boil water that turns into steam, which in turn drives an electricity-generating turbine.

Windmills of the future?
Wind power may be one answer to our energy needs for the future. These modern windmills, tall as a 10-story building, were designed by computer and built from lightweight metals and carbon fiber. Their power is used to generate electricity.

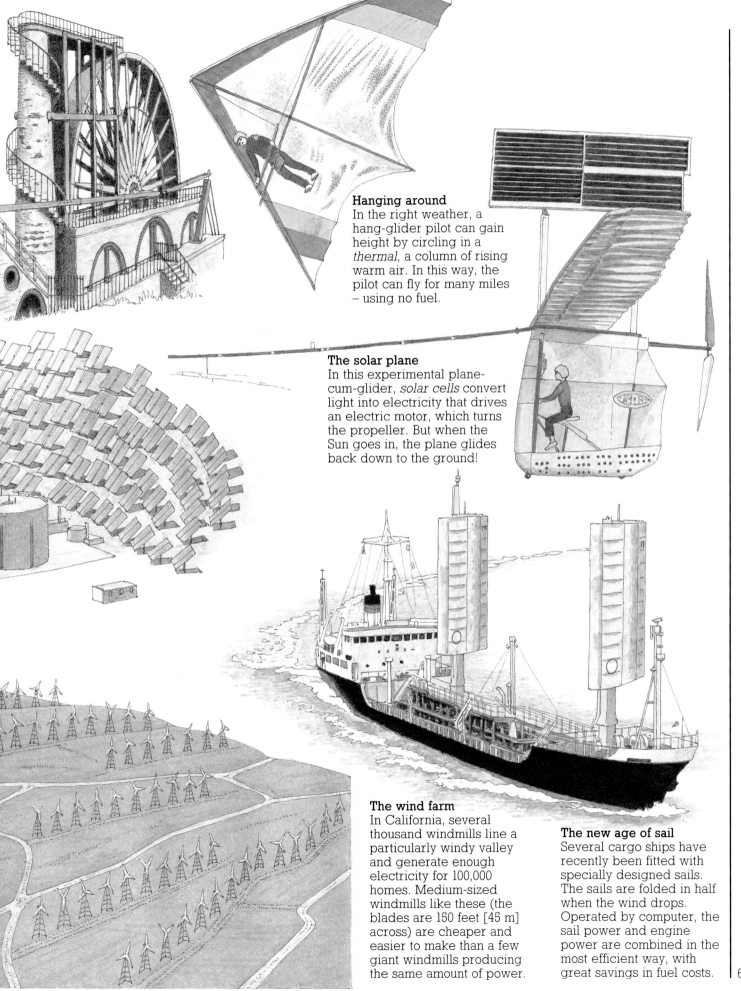

Hanging around
In the right weather, a hang-glider pilot can gain height by circling in a *thermal*, a column of rising warm air. In this way, the pilot can fly for many miles – using no fuel.

The solar plane
In this experimental plane-cum-glider, *solar cells* convert light into electricity that drives an electric motor, which turns the propeller. But when the Sun goes in, the plane glides back down to the ground!

The wind farm
In California, several thousand windmills line a particularly windy valley and generate enough electricity for 100,000 homes. Medium-sized windmills like these (the blades are 150 feet [45 m] across) are cheaper and easier to make than a few giant windmills producing the same amount of power.

The new age of sail
Several cargo ships have recently been fitted with specially designed sails. The sails are folded in half when the wind drops. Operated by computer, the sail power and engine power are combined in the most efficient way, with great savings in fuel costs.

GLOSSARY

(Words in *italics* have their own entries in the glossary.)

acid rain
Rain that has absorbed acidic gases in the air and can damage rocks and life.

asthenosphere
The part of the earth's *mantle* immediately below the lithosphere made of hot, molten rock.

atmosphere
The mixture of gases, clouds, and dust in the layer of "air" around the Earth.

axis
An imaginary line through the Earth on which the planet turns once each day like a wheel turning on an axle.

calcite
A clear or white *mineral* made from pure *calcium carbonate*.

calcium carbonate
A chemical molecule made of calcium, carbon, and oxygen ($CaCO_3$) found in *calcite*, chalk, and other *limestones*.

carbonic acid
The weak acid formed when water absorbs *carbon dioxide* gas from the *atmosphere*.

carbon dioxide
A colorless, odorless gas (CO_2) that makes up 1/3,000th of the *atmosphere*.

chromium
A natural chemical found in some *minerals*, such as rubies, that affects their color.

climate
The average weather conditions in an area over a long period of time.

condensation
When air cools and water vapor (a gas) turns into liquid water (the opposite of *evaporation).*

continent
One of the very large land masses on Earth (e.g. Africa or Australia).

core
The innermost part of Earth, partly solid and partly liquid.

corundum
A very hard *mineral* (aluminum and oxygen – Al_2O_3), sometimes found in the form of gems, such as rubies.

crust
The relatively thin outer layer of the Earth. Under the crust is the *mantle*.

currents, ocean
Large-scale movements of seawater resulting from the upper sea layers being heated by the Sun and the rotation of the Earth.

delta
The area of flat land, often triangle-shaped, through which a river runs into the sea (see also *estuary*).

equator
An imaginary line exactly halfway between the North and South poles, at right angles to the *axis*.

erosion
The gradual wearing away of the Earth's surface by rain, wind, ice, and so on.

estuary
Where a river widens out at its mouth and flows into the sea (see also *delta*).

evaporation
When water turns from being a liquid into a gas – water vapor (the opposite of *condensation*).

fluorine
A natural chemical found in some *minerals*, such as topaz, that affects their color.

geothermal
Heat from under the Earth's surface.

granite
A hard *igneous* rock made of three main *minerals*; mostly *quartz* and feldspar, with mica or hornblende.

gravitational
To do with gravity, the "pulling force" of any large body, such as the Earth.

hydroelectricity
Electricity made using the power of running water to spin a *turbine* and drive a generator.

The Earth mapped out
Shown here are the main continents (large land masses), subcontinents, and oceans of the world. Antarctica (the continent surrounding the South Pole) is shown on the small map on the far right. The technique of transferring the Earth's features to a flat sheet of paper is called a *projection*.

igneous
Rock that has heated up, melted, and then cooled and solidifed.

iridescence
A rainbowlike sheen on an object that changes color as the light shining on it alters.

limestone
A type of rock containing, among other substances, forms of *calcium carbonate* (lime).

lithospheric plate
One of the giant, curved, slowly moving, jigsawlike pieces that make up the Earth's surface.

manganese
A natural chemical found in some *minerals*, such as *quartz*, that affects their color.

magma
Molten rock far below the ground.

magnetic field
The invisible force around an object, such as the Earth, that attracts other objects to it.

manifold
A container built to withstand pressure, as around an *oil* well hole.

62

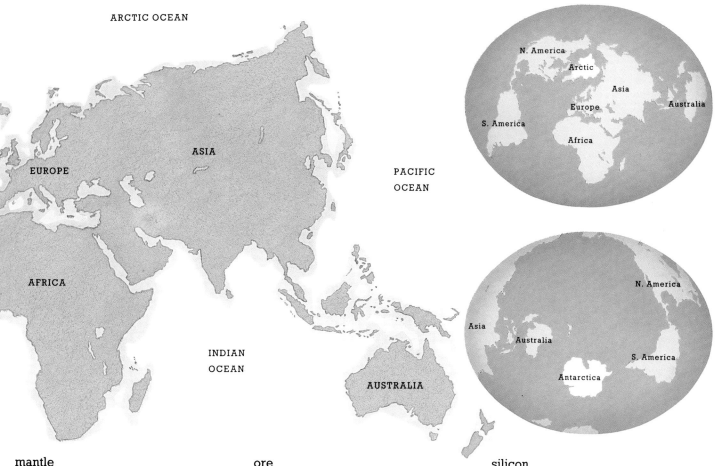

ARCTIC OCEAN

ASIA

EUROPE

AFRICA

PACIFIC OCEAN

INDIAN OCEAN

AUSTRALIA

N. America

Arctic

Asia

Europe

Australia

S. America

Africa

Asia

Australia

N. America

S. America

Antarctica

mantle
The middle layer of the Earth, between the *crust* and the *core.*

megawatt
A unit of power, often used for electricity. One megawatt equals one million watts (an ordinary light bulb is about 100 watts).

metamorphic
A type of rock that has been changed but not melted by great heat or pressure.

migration
The movement of animals, such as birds or antelopes, to another place on the Earth, usually with the seasons.

mineral
A natural, nonliving substance with a characteristic chemical makeup. For example, quartz is made from *silicon* and oxygen (silicon dioxide, SiO_2). Rocks are mixtures of minerals.

monsoon
The heavy rains that occur seasonally in and around the Indian Ocean.

oil
A naturally occurring fuel just below the Earth's surface, resulting from decayed plants and animals.

ore
A rock or *mineral* from which a valuable substance, such as a metal or gemstone, is obtained.

plankton
Microscopic creatures that drift in oceans, lakes, and rivers.

poles
The two opposite ends of the Earth's *axis*; they are known as the North Pole and the South Pole.

quartz
See *mineral.*

reef
An area of rock, mainly *limestone*, in shallow seawater, laid down over centuries by corals.

sandbar
A ridge of sand on the coast, formed by the action of wind, tides, and ocean *currents.*

sandstone
A type of rock formed from sand grains cemented together.

sedimentary
A type of rock formed when sediments, particles of sand and silt, collect, making a solid mass.

silicon
A chemical substance that is very common in rocks and forms *minerals*, such as quartz.

solar cell
A device that converts light (usually sunlight) into electricity.

sulfur
A common chemical substance. The gas sulfur dioxide dissolves in water in the *atmosphere* to form *acid rain.*

sunspot
A dark spot on the Sun's surface where the temperature is lower than elsewhere.

temperate
Between the *tropical* and the polar regions, where the *climate* is never extreme during the year, rarely very hot or very cold.

tropical
The zone around the Earth's *equator*, about 3,000 miles (5,100 km) wide, where the *climate* is warm all year.

turbine
A specially designed fan with many blades, spun efficiently by wind, water currents, exhaust gases, and so on (see *hydroelectricity*).

63

INDEX